The Language Report
English on the Move, 2000–2007

The Language Report

Susie Dent

PE
1872
.846
2007

OXFORD
UNIVERSITY PRESS

Great Clarendon Street, Oxford OX2 6DP

Oxford University Press is a department of the University of Oxford.
It furthers the University's objective of excellence in research, scholarship,
and education by publishing worldwide in

Oxford New York

Auckland Cape Town Dar es Salaam Hong Kong Karachi
Kuala Lumpur Madrid Melbourne Mexico City Nairobi
New Delhi Shanghai Taipei Toronto

With offices in

Argentina Austria Brazil Chile Czech Republic France Greece
Guatemala Hungary Italy Japan Poland Portugal Singapore
South Korea Switzerland Thailand Turkey Ukraine Vietnam

Oxford is a registered trademark of Oxford University Press
in the UK and in certain other countries

Published in the United States
by Oxford University Press Inc., New York

British Library Cataloguing in Publication Data

Data available

Library of Congress Cataloging in Publication Data

Data available

Typeset by Paul Saunders
Printed in Great Britain
by Clays Ltd, Bungay, Suffolk

ISBN 978-0-19-923388-5

For Lucy and Paul

Contents

Acknowledgements

Not one of Oxford's *language reports* has been the work of just one person. For each, a steadfast group of experts has guided me through the latest developments in their subjects so that the record of language change is as accurate and as current as we could make it. This book, the fifth *report*, is no exception—as before, I could not have managed without them.

The *language reports* are first and foremost a record of evidence collected by Oxford's language monitoring programme. Catherine Soanes and Angus Stevenson have mediated vast swathes of collected material in the course of the past five years; Catherine, in addition, has read each and every chapter and offered a hefty amount of advice as well as extra material in the process. Graeme Diamond, Michael Proffitt, Penny Silva, and many more at the *Oxford English Dictionary* have also been on hand with the very latest results of their tracking of English.

Grant Barrett, Orin Hargraves, Norman Gray, Andrew Ball, Jonathon Green, Paul Atkins, Rebecca Gowers, and Toby Murcott have all contributed to this new volume. This book owes much to their insights and ideas.

At OUP, Paul Saunders, Clare Jenkins, John Taylor and Nick Clarke have delivered creative design and production for all five *reports*. I also owe particular thanks to my commissioning editors Ben Harris and Judy Pearsall for their unobtrusive but unwavering support throughout.

Finally I have to thank Elizabeth Knowles for once again being a tirelessly supportive and inspiring consultant and contributor. Many of the best examples and discoveries in the *reports* are down to her.

Many thanks to all named here, and also to the hundreds of people who, unwittingly, provided me with some of the brightest words and phrases as I eavesdropped on their conversations, be it in a supermarket queue or among the students in the *Countdown* audience. My little black notebook has never been so handy.

Introduction

Bart (throwing gang symbols after hearing that top artists of hip hop are coming to Springfield): **Alcatraz is *widespread*! I'm talkin' da *junk*!**

Lisa (rolling her eyes): **Just what we need. Another lame suburban kid who loves rap.**

Bart: **So? You like the blues!**

Lisa (smugly): **Yeah, but the blues are *un*popular!**

Bart (more symbols): **Man, are you illin'!**

Lisa: **Rappers stopped saying *illin*' twelve years ago!**

Bart: **I'm keepin' it real!**

Lisa: **They stopped saying *keepin' it real* three years ago.**

Bart: **Mom, Lisa's dissin' me!**

Marge: **Dissin'? Do rappers still say that?**

> From 'Pranksta Rap', an episode of *The Simpsons*, 2005.

The aim of each *language report* has been to monitor the shifting language scene, to record its changes and the new words it produces, and to probe the reasons behind those changes. This, the fifth *report*, is no different. As ever, there is a rich pool of neologisms from which to select the words that are most resonant of the year we have lived through. And, almost eight years into the new century, there is an equally strong argument for looking back, and for judging whether the predictions each one of us made at the start have come true. History, however short in span, can be as instructive about our future direction as the present. This seems particularly true in the case of English.

The beginning of the new millennium was marked by intense speculation about our future. Fears of a meltdown of the world's computers, wrought by the dawn of **Y2K** at one minute past midnight, anxieties about growing unrest in the Middle East, predictions by the media about developments in almost every human activity, from the new goals in space exploration to the hottest celebrities of the new **noughties**—all suggested that a time of great change was upon us; the start of a new epoch for mankind.

The first *language report*, published in 2003, reflected a continued sense of anticipation, fuelled by the dramatic events of war. That year's new words and phrases reflected that drama, as well as a return to political pessimism after the bullish buoyancy of the nineties. Five years on, the language recorded for this fifth *report* suggests, in some areas at least, a rather different sense of anticipation. As political terms of office ended (and went on ending, in the case of the British premiership), and the continuing conflict in Iraq provoked serious misgivings about earlier decisions, the feeling in 2007 became more one of limbo than of change. Linguistically as well as on the ground, the predictions of great change may not have been entirely justified.

In some areas, of course, there has been a very real sense of transformation. The realities of global warming have made **green**, as the *New York Times* put it, the colour of the new century. Preoccupations with our **carbon footprint** ('carbon' being among the biggest generators of new word combinations in 2007) have had a significant impact on our daily vocabulary. Even as the typescript for this *report* was handed over, the phrase **chip and bin** was a matter of furious debate. Slang too, as it always does, has moved on with reliable regularity. As the above excerpt from *The Simpsons* (a great source of linguistic creativity) shows, slang moves on almost as soon as it is documented—that, after all, is its aim. It is therefore a surprise that most of the slang we encounter is in fact rather old: like so much of our language, it is recycled and remoulded by new generations who somehow manage to make it sound completely new (**illing**, dismissed by Lisa Simpson, was reborn in rap in the 1980s: its sense of behaving badly can in fact be dated back to the 1500s).

At the start of the century, the influence on English of online technology looked likely to be dramatic. And so it has proved. While every new technology has shaped our language—from printing to the postcard—the measure to which the Internet and mobile phone have done so is probably unprecedented. Change in this area was guaranteed. And yet it is the nature of that change which has proved somewhat unexpected. Communicating wirelessly is now so much the norm that linguistic creativity looks to be slowing down: being 'offline' is the exception rather than the rule, and 'online' is no longer the novelty it once was. Certainly, there are still numerous communities—of bloggers, chatroom visitors, and game-players—who are endlessly inventive with their own lexicons, but most of today's 'online' English is just as likely to be used in or about our daily concrete world as in our exclusively virtual experiences.

The absorption of other Englishes into our own, evident for some time now, has gathered momentum in this new opening decade. Many linguists predict that **Hinglish**, a hybrid of Hindi and English and the hippest language on the streets of India, will extend its influence across the English-speaking world, while Black English continues to add the strongest flavours to British and American slang, as it has done since the Second World War. It is rap and hip-hop in particular that we can thank for some of the brightest idioms in current English, including **ghostriding the whip** and **catching the vapours** (this last example, from the very first *report*, means simply to be caught up in someone else's popularity, the desire perhaps of many in the new **sleb**-obsessed world). Not all words are up for grabs, however: in 2007, the US 'shock jock' Don Imus was fired for harnessing the rap term **ho**, while the treatment of Shilpa Shetty led to loud accusations of racism inside and outside the *Big Brother* house. Both episodes reignited the debate about cultural taboos and demonstrated that, even in 2007, there remain many words that are considered unacceptable.

The likely influences of war, new technologies, other Englishes, and politics upon language change were all clearly predicted as the new century began. Equally, the signs of a 'green' revolution were already there, even if it had not yet been fully catalysed. At the time of the first *language report*, however, there were the early rumblings of a new trend which few had foreseen: the rise of a distinct 'us and them' mentality which in turn led to a new register of social labels. From **chavs** to **hoodies** and the apparent return of the **Sloanes**, commentary on the people around us became a free-for-all without the self-censorship applied to other areas of sensitivity, such as race and ethnicity. In 2007 and with the news of Prince William's split from his girlfriend (at the time) Kate Middleton, the terms **U** and **non-U**, popularized by Nancy Mitford in the 1950s, made a surprise return to currency.

For many, this new and explicit rejection of certain groups coincided with a withdrawal of freedom for those suspected of political rather than social crimes. One result was measures as extreme as the euphemistically phrased **extraordinary rendition**, Salman Rushdie's choice for ugliest phrase of 2006. Analysis of the linguistic evidence collected by Oxford as part of a vast database of current English (the Oxford English Corpus) shows an exponential increase during the 2000s of the vocabulary of surveillance and security.

Five years worth of recording some of the new words of each year, charted in the 'Bubbling Under' category (to borrow a phrase from the music industry), offers a good deal of insight into both our changing and our continuing preoccupations. There have been some spectacular winners, from **bling**, **metrosexual** (and the whole string of epithets it sparked), and **blogs** (and **vlogs**, **phlogs**, and **splogs**), to **bird flu** and **jumping the couch**. All of them tell their own story. The losers are for the most part less dramatic, and come from many sources—**bromances**, **mandals**, and **cuddle parties** fizzled a little too soon. As for the neologisms of 2007, it is too early to tell, but one can hope that **flipping**, **starshades**, and **prevenge** all get a run for their money.

All five *language reports* have been written at a time when English is noted more for its decline than its vitality. Reports of plummeting standards of grammar and of a shrinking teen vocabulary have convinced us that the golden age of our language will forever be situated in the past. In fact, the summary picture presented in these records suggests the very opposite: that creativity is thriving in a language which is proving its robustness by its very ability to adapt. Certainly good English needs to be championed and fought for— but 'good' surely denotes a language that is articulately expressed and readily understood by its hearers, not one reflecting an adherence to principles that are no longer appropriate in this new world. Splendid diversity has characterized our language through-out its 1,500-year history. If we can predict little else, we can at least anticipate a continuation of that growth and variation. The main purpose of each *language report* has been to reflect some of the many reasons to celebrate: together the picture they present is very far from black. Whatever else is going on around us, English, without doubt, will never be in limbo.

Susie Dent
October 2007

words in the spotlight

1

2000–2007:
The Winners and the Losers

'The history of new words,' Allan Metcalf writes in *Predicting New Words* (2002), his study of neologisms and the secrets of their success, 'is largely a tale of failure.' Over the course of the 20th century, the *Oxford English Dictionary* records approximately 90,000 new words, and new meanings of old words, which came into English in that time. In other words, each year on average 900 neologisms made a sufficient mark as to be considered established in the language.

While those 90,000 coinages reflect an enormous expansion of English over those 100 years, what the figure cannot reflect are the many thousands of new words and senses which were legitimate creations but which failed to win an almost Darwinian struggle of survival and prove themselves the fittest. In other words, they did not have sufficient currency to gain a place in the *OED*. Modern lexicographers apply strict criteria to each new word which comes their way: only a handful of all those they see will become serious candidates for inclusion in their dictionary.

In the 2000s (or the *noughties*, *oughties*, or *zips*), a newly-minted word has had an unprecedented opportunity to be heard beyond its original creator. With 24-hour media coverage, and the infinite space of the Internet, the chain of ears and mouths has never been longer, and the repetition of a new word today takes a fraction of the time it would have taken a hundred, or even fifty, years ago. If, then, only the smallest percentage of new words make it into current dictionaries, what are the determining factors in their success?

Very roughly speaking, there are five primary contributors to the survival of a new word: usefulness, user-friendliness, exposure, the durability of the subject it describes, and its potential associations or extensions. If a new word fulfils these robust criteria it stands a very good chance of inclusion in the modern lexicon.

The war lexicon

Words are servants of events. Some of the most striking new words of this century have emerged from dramatic events, saturation coverage of which has imprinted them in public memory. The first *language report*, published in 2003, inevitably contained much about the vocabulary of war. For all their destruction, wars, paradoxically, seem to have a generative effect on language. Each major war has had its own vocabulary: World War I produced **shellshocked** and **no man's land**, World War II **jeep** and **firestorm**, while **brainwash**, **fallout**, and **friendly fire** were the survivors from Korea, the Cold War, and Vietnam respectively. In 2003, the second war in Iraq catalysed new forms of military jargon which were used so insistently by the reporters (who, for the first time, were **embedded** within the ranks of the soldiers on the frontline, thus ensuring that we saw and heard more of the war than any other non-combatants before us) that newspapers published glossaries decoding the new vocabulary.

Of the hundreds of new words to emerge during the conflict, some were resurrected from a distant past because they had suddenly acquired a new resonance. Thomas Aquinas and the Schoolmen

mbedded **friendly fire** jeep **oughties** brainwash **zips** bra discussed the criteria for a *justum bellum* in medieval times: over 700 years later George Bush Jr. spoke of a **just war** in defence of a pre-emptive strike, thereby prompting heated debate. Equally prominent in the US government's rhetoric was the argument of a **moral crusade** (designed to counter the threat from the **axis of evil,** represented by those countries whose governments posed the biggest threat to **homeland security**). In the 21st century, however, 'crusade' is a loaded term. Shortly afterwards the Bush administration dropped the term. Perhaps Bush's speechwriters had reached for the words of an earlier President—in 1944 Franklin Roosevelt had addressed the nation on D-Day and spoken of 'faith in our united crusade'—while overlooking the cultural change that nearly 60 years had brought.

Meanwhile, new terms for killing, a natural target for euphemism throughout history, also emerged during a war which itself was often referred to as **constructive engagement**. The verbs **degrading**, **deconflicting**, and **attriting** were all synonyms for killing in battle. Meanwhile, in the detention centre of Guantanamo Bay, the term *prisoner of war* was controversially replaced by that of **unlawful combatant**, a phrase seen by many commentators as a means of avoiding the strictures of the Geneva Convention regarding the proper treatment of prisoners of war. A similar legal loophole was said to be sought in the process of **extraordinary rendition**, referring to the top-secret capture and 'outsourcing' of terrorists for what many assumed was interrogation via torture.

Out of the direct battle zone, the conflict had ramifications which extended far beyond anyone's expectations. Contesting for the phrase of 2003 was the term **sexing up**, infamously used to describe the alleged **dodgy dossier** compiled by Tony Blair's government to bolster support for war (a dossier which had prompted Britain's *Sun* newspaper to declare: 'Brits 45 Mins from Doom'). As **weapons of mass destruction** (or **WMDs**) proved elusive, accusations against the government accumulated daily. The death of the Ministry of Defence official David Kelly only underscored the importance of language both in rationalizing war and in reporting it. The most dramatic encounters between historic events and language can occur when words become direct agents of change as well as descriptors.

Can all of the above words and phrases born out of political and social events be termed winners? Certainly each of them amply fulfils the first of the dictionary editor's criteria: each proved useful to their originators and to those who latched onto them as potent descriptors of the events unfolding around them. As a result, the second criterion—of exposure—was guaranteed. The versatility and user-friendliness of many of the terms was also not in doubt: *weapons of mass destruction* was harnessed by sources as varied as tabloid headline writers describing their page 3 pinups, and sports journalists reporting on one football team's annihilation by another. That leaves one criterion to consider, namely the durability of the context to which all these terms are attached.

Durability in this case can be defined quite broadly, for it concerns not just the lifetime of the event or context itself, but its importance in a historical context. Even if the events themselves are 'completed' and succeeded by others, their impact can be long-lasting. Words often provide historians with a powerful distillation of the event they are recording. Language can provide such an immediate summary of an event that a single word or phrase can become its shorthand. The original context of the term is never quite lost, so that all subsequent uses are underpinned by that original reference point.

dossier **extraordinary rendition** just war **moral crusade**

A number of the event-driven words and phrases from the conflict in Iraq possess such power. *Dodgy dossier* was a phrase which arose from a very specific use which was then endlessly picked over by the media and repeated widely. It is unlikely to ever shake off the events which generated it. The US administration's *moral crusade* and *axis of evil* are likely to be as permanently attached to the war as the code names given to the battles within it. Equally, *unlawful combatant* and *extraordinary rendition* are likely to retain some of the tarnish left by the controversy they prompted.

These seemingly inextricable links between word and event do not indicate a linguistic failure to run free: rather for many they demonstrate the power of language to convey, in a very short space, a complex array of historical associations. One mention today of the word **tsunami**, a term until recently largely confined to the vocabulary of seismologists and geographers, is likely to evoke for millions the very specific and shocking effects of the events in Asia in the closing days of 2004. Similarly, few of us will associate **ground zero** with anything other than the site on which New York's Twin Towers previously stood. The term's previous (and relatively long) history as a designation of the hole left in the earth by an atomic bomb has been almost entirely supplanted, such is the power of the word's new association.

Terms such as these, even when the events with which they are linked fade from view, are likely to resonate for many years to come. Other words, meanwhile, may shake off their origins and move with assurance into our general vocabulary. The new sense of *embed*, born in the very same moment in history, is likely to be used in military contexts for years to come, irrespective of the battle in discussion. As such, it too has almost certainly proved itself a winner, albeit in a more anonymous way.

nd zero **axis of evil** tsunami **embed** ground zero axis of e

The typecasting trend

The exposure ensured for words born out of major political and social events is certainly a powerful factor in their success. Other neologisms have to rely on other catalysts for gaining public attention. The 21st century has provided many examples of words which have succeeded through their own momentum in gaining enormous profile, some of them spectacularly so. For many observers of language there is one word which, perhaps more than any other, has the unmistakable stamp of modern Britain, and which, however disagreeable its application, would be a leading candidate for the word of the century thus far. In 2004, **chav** propelled itself into the public arena; it has stayed there ever since. Used to describe both an individual and an entire social class, the force with which it entered our daily vocabulary, and the intense debate surrounding it, provided a near-perfect example of modern linguistic success. 'Chav' was elected the word of the year in the *language report* of 2004: its selection prompted headlines across broadsheets and tabloids announcing (and regretting) the arrival of a perceived underclass with no taste or social graces.

The phenomenon of 'chav' was probably started by the website *chavscum.co.uk*, a site presenting itself as 'a humorous guide to Britain's burgeoning peasant underclass'. It was taken up by users of the irreverent celebrity-gossip bulletin board *popbitch.com*, many of whom work in the media. It was from the outset an offensive term, the British equivalent of the US's *white* or *trailer trash* and described by one commentator in the *Guardian* as a label for 'the non-respectable working classes: the dole-scroungers, petty criminals, football hooligans and teenage pram-pushers'. The fashion choices of the 'chav' were also denounced: baseball caps, trainers, branded shirts and jackets, and flashy jewellery. Female

se facelift **chav** council house facelift **chavtastic** chavspot *chavs*, or *chavettes*, displayed a tightly drawn pony tail otherwise known as the **council house facelift**. A whole lexicon based on the term 'chav' quickly emerged: **chavspotting** became a pastime promoted on many a blog and website which found the whole game **chavtastic**.

The trajectory that *chav* has taken is an interesting one. Clearly a term of abuse, its edges nonetheless began to blur over time: so much so that major fashion labels were said to be considering explicitly labelled 'chav' fashion lines to tap into what they saw as a new—and presumably desirable—trend. Manuals on how to be a 'chav' appeared in the bookshops, and uses of the term began to fall into two camps: the one resolutely hostile, and the other tongue-in-cheek. In 2007, however, that began to change, and *chav* looks again to be seen as the demonization of a whole group of people at the bottom of the social ladder (see 'Us and Them', pp 47–54). The nastiness of *chav*, it seemed, may have become more acute than ever.

'Chav' can certainly be regarded as a winner in the linguistic sense: dramatically so, in fact. The meteoric rise of the term suggested very strongly that it was brand new. In fact, 'chav' seems likely to be over 150 years old, and to stem from the Romany word *chavi* which originally designated a child before it became a term of insult towards an adult man. Its geographical (and some experts believe its etymological) origins are in Chatham, Kent. Today's use of the term recognizes only social rather than local boundaries.

Social definition, probably because of the 'chav' debate, has been a major talking point in the 2000s. The 'chav' sits alongside **Trobos**, **hoods**, **neds**, **charvers**, **spides**, **nobs**, and **gudgeons**, terms which for the most part have remained local dialect labels for various

white trash chav **chavette** chavtastic **chavspotting** cour 'tribes'. They are all part of a much wider discussion about general social malaise and what David Cameron termed 'decivilized' behaviour: evident from the apparent failure of **ASBO**s, an acronym for 'anti-social behaviour orders' which has nonetheless been a linguistic winner; even **BASBO**s—'baby' ASBOs for very young offenders—were mooted as a possibility.

Social categorization has not stopped there. The early 21st century saw a line of new types emerge in quick succession, including **metrosexuals** (men who spend a lot of time on their appearance), **machosexuals** and **retrosexuals** (men who do not), **übersexuals** (representing a return to unashamed masculinity, of the caring kind), **ecosexuals** (single and environmentally conscious individuals), and **contrasexuals** (women who shun traditional expectations of femininity). The **ladult** was the term of choice for a man laddish in behaviour but able to show maturity when required. The phenomenon of children remaining financially dependent on their parents well into adulthood spawned a further new category of terms, including **kidults** and **boomerang kids**. Revenge may be taken by those parents who become **skiers**—perhaps a symptom of **middlescence**—by choosing instead to go and 'spend their kids' inheritance'.

s hoods spides ladults ASBO BASBO kidults retrosexual

Bling it on

Few other words can rival 'chav' in the speed and force with which it embedded itself in daily discourse. As the century opened, however, another term suggested itself as the likely word of the noughties and it, too, was not without social and class connotations. If it has receded somewhat in the last year or two, few who hear it today will be confused by it. **Bling** (or **bling-bling**) is so powerful a word that it packs a host of associations which no other word could convey. As such it fulfils a major criterion for a successful neologism: it was needed.

Although much associated with the 21st century, *bling* was in fact first recorded in print in 1998, as a song title by US rapper B.G. ('Baby Gangsta'). Used to refer to ostentatiously expensive clothing or jewellery, or the style or attitudes associated with them, it was probably suggested by the idea of light reflecting off a diamond, or by the sound of jewellery clashing together. It quickly and steadily moved out of the hip-hop world and into the mainstream in Britain as well as America, acquiring along the way a whole range of variants and uses.

Bling became journalists' favourite way of summing up our supposedly over-materialistic, celebrity-obsessed society at the beginning of the 21st century, much as Harry Enfield's catchphrase 'Loadsamoney!' remains popular British shorthand for the booming Thatcherite eighties. *Bling* now functions as a noun, an adjective, and a verb, and has generated numerous spin-off words such as **bling-blingy**, **un-bling**, and **blinger**. In each of these it denotes something vulgar and showy. If its time is passing (**post-bling** is now in currency), and a new word will emerge to sum up the next big social trend, *bling-bling* will live on as a term that instantly evokes the early 2000s.

achosexuals **neds** bling **spides** ladults **ASBO** BASBO kidu

Technologically speaking

While things *bling* were considered cheap and rather trashy, the word itself has not suffered any equivalent kind of linguistic snobbery. Not so **blog**, a spectacularly successful creation which has taken off dramatically over the last three years but which has been criticized for its ugliness (see 'Jottings and Musings', pp 81–2). The word is a contraction of 'web log', and designates an online journal which is intended for public consumption and which is designed so that its readers can interact with the blog-keeper. During the Iraq conflict the blogs of those Iraqis witnessing the war at first hand were often compulsive reading—and a source of information for the media at home.

Blog was coined in 1997, but made its impact much later. It admirably meets the criterion of versatility, having spawned an entire lexicon which plays on its name. Today we can make virtual visits to **vlogs**, **phlogs**, and **clogs** (video, photo, and camera logs), complain of **splogs**—spam or fake blogs which contain links affiliated to the keeper of the blog, thereby attracting more visitors—or simply roam the **blogosphere**. However crude an invention in linguistic terms, *blog* has certainly made its mark.

Podcasting, a leading contender for the word of 2004, shares many of *blog*'s characteristics and echoes much of its history. Podcasting is the broadcasting or downloading of audio broadcasts via an *iPod*, a portable music player produced by Apple Incorporated. It too is a 'portmanteau' word, a blend of 'iPod' and 'broadcasting', and, like *blog*, it quickly generated a subset of associated words: **mommy-casting** denotes downloads made by and aimed at mothers; **couple-casting** is a programme presented by a couple and which often discusses relationship issues; while **Godcasting** is the broadcasting or downloading of religious content. **Vodcasting** and **blogcasting** are video and blog broadcasts made available for downloading.

Staying with technology, the search engine Google has seen its name become the top generic term of choice for searching on the Internet. To **google** is certainly among the biggest winners of the last decade. Looking to the future, it may well be that **youtube** as a verb, meaning to look at something on the *YouTube* site or to post video content on it, will also emerge: indeed, Google itself already shows over a hundred verbal uses of the company it acquired in 2007.

Tongue in cheek?

War, technology, and social labelling were at the forefront of neologizing in the 21st century. But not all new words were quite so serious. Wordplay has for centuries been at the heart of many coinages, and it is one of the many processes in the evolution of language which shows no sign of slowing down. Among the many new 'blends' of the last five years have been **waparazzi**, those members of the public who imitate the paparazzi and take pictures of celebrities with their (WAP-enabled) mobile phones; **blooks** (books published in serialized form on web logs: *blogs*, it seems, are hard to escape); and **chofas** (a cross between a chair and a sofa). Humour softened the undesirability of a **muffin top**, that area of flesh which protrudes above a pair of low-slung trousers (**hipsters** or **bumsters**), and the trademark shape of a **whale tail** (a visible thong). **Yummy mummies** meanwhile became the leaders of new fashion, even if their cars of choice, **Chelsea tractors**, have attracted much criticism as well as the threat of extra taxes. At the other end of the fashion and social spectrum, **hoodies**, a term which now designates those teenagers who wear hooded sweatshirts as well

azzi **chofa** yummy mummy **hoodie** bovvered **WAG** galact as the garments themselves, have come to symbolize an entire generation of disaffected youth (characterized by their catchphrase **bovvered**, the 2006 *language report*'s word of the year).

In the summer of 2006, it was the word **WAG** which was making the headlines: the exploits of the English World Cup football team's 'wives and girlfriends' seemed to be rivalling the on-pitch efforts of their partners. *WAG* provided a model example of the way in which modern media, and in particular tabloid headline-writers, can cement a new word in the public lexicon within hours. *WAG* soon filtered out into journalistic coverage of other football teams and beyond, into the world of politicians and musicians. It retains however a particular resonance in the world of **galacticos**, the football superstars whose wives and girlfriends, for the tabloids at least, vie for the media spotlight. 'Schoolgirl chav to gladrag WAG' was the *Sun's* verdict on Coleen McLoughlin, fiancée of Wayne Rooney.

*WAG*s and *galacticos* were not the only contributions from the world of football to our daily vocabulary. In 2004 an energetic bid was made for an improbable-sounding new word to be included in future dictionaries of current English. **Bouncebackability** was a term thought to have been coined by the manager of the English football club Crystal Palace, Ian Dowie, when he announced that 'Crystal Palace have shown great bouncebackability against their opponents to be really back in this game'. The word was picked up by Sky TV's *Soccer AM* programme, who noticed the frequency of the word in post-match quotes from players and managers since Dowie's original (in fact, the *OED* can ante-date Dowie's use by as many as 40 years, although he can certainly be credited with popularizing it). A petition was subsequently launched for the word to gain inclusion in the *Concise Oxford Dictionary*. Evidence of the

bouncebackability bumsters chofa waparazzi hoodie bo

likely longevity of the word meant that *bouncebackability* did indeed go into the dictionary in 2006.

The speed at which new words travel today is indisputably greater than at any time in English's history. The importance of speed in other respects was reflected in a number of new trends to emerge that cater to our modern hectic and soundbite-friendly society. **Speeddating** and **speedfriending**, in which potential mates are sought at parties where each attendee has a few minutes with a series of contenders, were big news in the early 2000s, as were, perhaps rather more cynically, **Botox parties**.

Idioms too can be winning formulae, and their origins are often worth exploring. In 2006, Tom Cruise suddenly and dramatically jumped up and down on the sofa of US chat show host Oprah Winfrey during an interview about his new love for Katie Holmes. Such random and erratic behaviour deserved, in the eyes of those who witnessed it, a term of its own, and so **jumping the couch** was born. Before long George Bush was also said to have 'jumped the couch' in his actions in Iraq. The idiom, striking as it was, was in fact based on the model of an idiom from the 1990s which may possibly outlive its successor. **Jumping the shark** denotes the point at which a successful TV programme, or indeed any venture, begins to go downhill. It was coined in response to an episode (considered to be far-fetched) of the TV series *Happy Days*, in which the main character, the Fonz, jumps over a shark while waterskiing. Viewing figures after that were said to have gone into a rapid decline. Meanwhile an idiom which has crossed over from the advertising of a single product to common use in any number of contexts is **it does exactly what it says on the tin**. The makers of Ronseal wood protector no doubt delight in its slogan's progression, which now includes allusions to people as well as objects.

The darker side

The language of disease has also, unfortunately, been a source of several high-profile coinages in recent years. In 2006, the **H5N1** virus became the latest threat to public health and an unlikely candidate for the list of prominent new words of 2006. Like its recent predecessor **SARS** in 2004, the term lodged itself in the public mind in spite of its cold unmemorability. A scientific formula seemed to have a more portentous ring than **bird flu**, possibly because the latter became the subject of so much black humour. Perhaps the linguistic middle ground was to be found in a further equivalent, **avian flu** (or **AI**, 'avian influenza'), which brought the hitherto rather specialized term *avian* into common usage, much as *tsunami* had become the year before.

Unlike *H5N1*, *SARS* (an acronym for 'severe acute respiratory syndrome') had no vernacular equivalent. While it was quickly taken up by the world's media—so readily was the term adopted in Britain that the tabloid newspapers felt confident enough to use it in punning headlines such as 'SARS WARS'—it has faded from public memory thanks to the demise of the disease, at least for now. Like **Y2K** (see overleaf), it served its purpose for a short period of time.

nners Botox party speeddating bird flu SARS jumping th

The losers

It would be an impossible task for a lexicographer to pinpoint all those words which failed to make a sufficiently strong or lasting mark on the language to warrant inclusion in the next edition of their dictionary. Thousands of neologisms, however creative and colourful, simply do not gain the wide exposure or approval required. It is precisely because of this lack of exposure that we are largely unaware of those coinages which failed to thrive.

Nonetheless there are some words which looked very likely to become winners in the 21st-century lexicon but which, often for good reason but sometimes inexplicably, never quite made it. Perhaps the most common factor in their demise is that the very thing or event they describe is no longer topical or relevant. The term **millennium bug**, due to hit at the beginning of the new millennium or **Y2K**, was one of the most frequently Googled items in the closing months of 1999, and the threat it described caused enormous alarm across the computer-based business world. In the event, the calamities predicted failed to materialize, and both terms had virtually disappeared within just a few weeks after the start of the new century. Whether such items can truly be categorized as 'losers' is open to debate, but their very specifity means they will not outlive the context they were coined to describe.

The following list includes just a handful of those words which flew above the radar and then disappeared off the lexical screen:

slacktivism: the desire to do something good as long as it involves minimal effort. The term, a contraction of *slack* and *activism*, was one of many new recent 'blends', including **blipvert** (= *blip* + *advert*), **flexecutive** (= *flexible* + *executive*), and **webisode** (= *Web* + *episode)*, a short film available exclusively on the Web.

third (of a pint, designed for women): a long-stemmed beer glass carrying a third of a pint, plans for which were launched in 2005 by the British Beer and Pub Association as part of a campaign to present beer to women as an alternative to wine. The Association believed that women would find traditional half or full pint glasses too heavy. A *Times* article discussing the idea was headed 'Does my beer look big in this?'

furkid: a pet which serves as a child substitute. The term was a successor to 'animal guardian' and 'furbaby', both of which emerged in the 1990s. 'Furkid' was used by some animal lovers who feel that the word 'pet' suggests the idea of owning something rather than describing the loving relationship that they have with their dog, cat, etc.

popstrology: the theory that the hit song of the day, month, and year on which a person is born influences their character.

happy slapping: this brutal and occasionally fatal pursuit of mugging or hitting an innocent passer-by and having an accomplice record the deed on their mobile phone hit the headlines in 2005. It has, fortunately, rather receded from view, although other unpalatable mobile phone pursuits have taken their place.

to dyson: this verb has been expected to enter the language as a rival for 'hoovering' for some years. As yet, however, it has failed to make any impact.

heart (as a verb, usually translated as a ♥ symbol): in most news-papers and online accounts the heart symbol in the 2005 film title *I ♥ Huckabees* was transcribed as 'heart'. While not the first instance of the use of the heart symbol (graffiti and bumper stickers bearing the legend I ♥ NY/CA/my cat etc. have, for example, been around since the 1970s or earlier), the film briefly sparked off a succession of uses of 'heart' as a verb, meaning simply 'to love' ('I heart my boo').

memail: an email sent purely to gain attention. The term may be related to the search engine Google's personalized email service MeMail.

bromance (a blend of 'brother' and 'romance'): a non-sexual relationship between men, particularly in the first 'rush' of a new friendship. A meeting between such men is known as a **man date**.

quillow: a cross between a quilt and a pillow. Like many similar terms invented by businesses or marketing companies, (including **togethering**, spending quality time with one's **framily**, or friends and family, and **mancation**, an all-male holiday) it failed to establish itself in any generic way.

yeppie: an acronym for a young, experimenting perfection-seeker. This was just one of many acronyms coined as labels for social types, the flag-bearer for which was the **yuppie** of the 80s. The 2000s have also seen come and go **smanker** (single, middle-aged, no kids), **yettie** (young, entrepreneurial technocrat), and **skier** (spender of one's kids' inheritance).

textonym: in 2006 it was hoped that textonyms would become an important new form of text slang. In predictive texting, key-combinations often correspond to several different words: so 5477 can, appropriately, render both 'kiss' and 'lips', or 686 may be 'nun' or 'mum'. These 'text synonyms' were dubbed 'textonyms' (or txto-nyms). In this new version of 'textspeak', 'book' became the latest by-word for 'cool', and friends began to be asked out for a 'riot' rather than a 'pint': both words are the first choices by the software for the combinations in question. If taken further, the result would have fulfilled the most important criterion of slang: that as a spoken code it takes some time for outsiders to crack. Sadly, textonyms look to have been far more fleeting a trend than promised.

binikis (also known as **butt-bras**)**:** a support device for the buttocks designed to give them a firm shape.

marmalade dropper: a news item in a morning paper which is so shocking that it causes the reader to drop their breakfast toast. The US equivalent was a **muffin choker**.

cuddle parties: an American invention, these were parties at which attendees were invited to indulge in physical but non-sexual contact, as a way of engendering positive feelings of wellbeing. While many newspapers enjoyed the idea, few of their readers took it up.

grey goo: a hypothetical catastrophe feared by some scientists and involving millions of tiny molecular nano-robots replicating themselves and rapidly annihilating life on earth. The word came under the spotlight after Prince Charles warned of the dangers of nanotechnology in 2004, even though the Prince didn't actually use the term himself.

freedom fries: a short-lived name used by some in the United States as a substitute for French fries. They were said to be served on the US Presidential flights during the run-up to the 2003 invasion of Iraq, and were the result of anti-French sentiment caused by a perceived lack of support for the war from the French government.

freeganism: a philosophy or moral system whose followers source as much food as possible from rubbish that has been thrown out by supermarkets, restaurants, and street markets. The practice is also known as **voluntary simplicity** or **ethical eating**, and is intended as a statement of defiance against what 'freegans' regard as the wasteful consumerist culture of the developed world.

taikonaut: a Chinese astronaut. The word derives from the Chinese *tai kong*, meaning outer space.

TMI: text message injury (to the hands and fingers, the result of too much texting).

twobicle: a women's toilet cubicle for two people.

Enronomics: a dubious accounting policy or business strategy, used by Democrats to criticize Republican spending policies and in the wake of the collapse of the multi-billion dollar corporation Enron which had issued false accounts.

concestor: a common ancestor of man. The term was coined by the scientist Richard Dawkins in his book *The Ancestor's Tale* (2004), but has not moved out beyond his work.

2
Bigger Brother

Our immersion in language is not unlike our immersion in family or community: companionship is so continuous that small and subtle changes in the surroundings may slip by unnoticed. On an abstract level we are aware that nothing endures but change, but for the most part, we absorb changes to our language without questioning them and, in many cases, instinctively and without a mental check.

The development of the Oxford English Corpus (OEC) during the early years of the 21st century, culminating in its release in 2006, gave linguists and other language-watchers a new tool for observing small and subtle changes in language: changes of the kind that might go unnoticed but for minute observation or sudden insight. Looking at usage patterns in English with the aid of this unprecedentedly complete and broadly-based repository of contemporary language (at the last count, it contained 1.5 billion words) provides an opportunity to track and document trends in the way people write and talk that might otherwise be supportable only by impressions or anecdotes. The Corpus is essentially a database of current language: into it are fed journals, newspapers, novels, blogs, transcriptions of chat-room and street conversations—in fact as broad a selection possible of English as it is really used by all of us today.

onaut freeganism TMI concestor twobicle The Losers ta

Pared down to its essentials, the Oxford English Corpus is information. The English language in the 21st century is preoccupied with information, simply because its speakers and writers are preoccupied with it (or alternatively, deluged, flummoxed, and defeated by it). While few would argue that the information age is a phenomenon that began in the 21st century—indeed, some put its inception in the 19th century, with the invention of the telegraph and telephone—this century has seen a proliferation of information, along with tools for its transmission, expansion, compaction, storage, retrieval, and manipulation. So much so in fact that our discourse about it barely keeps pace with the actual changes. Tracking some of the patterns of changing usage in the OEC during the opening years of the century, 2000–2006, brings some of these changes to light.

The linguist J.R. Firth, writing in 1957, is credited with a phrase which is very apt for the study of the language held in a corpus: 'You shall know a word by the company it keeps.' The company kept by a number of information-related words has undergone significant changes this century. A theme growing ever more pervasive is that of information as a consumable. As if to set the stage for the daily engorgement of data that we now enjoy, software analyst Rachel Chalmers, writing in the *New Scientist* in 2000, noted that 'We're all informavores now, hunting down and consuming data as our ancestors once sought woolly mammoths and witchetty grubs.' A statistical analysis of the verb **digest** in the year 2000 finds it with various objects: *food*, as you might expect, comes near the top of words which co-occur with it; *information*, on the other hand, comes very close to the bottom. Five years later, in 2005, *information* ranks second to *food* in the things that we are in the habit of digesting.

One word with a very long association with food is, appropriately, **feed**. Back in the 16th century, *feed* meant food for cattle and other creatures, a meaning of course it still possesses. In the 19th century, *feed* moved on in a natural way to denote the steady input of a commodity or material to an industrial machine, and by the process of metonymy, or substitution, it soon denoted the material itself: thus, the feed to a boiler, loom, or printing press.

The 20th century saw the development of the satellite or broadcast feed: the steady stream of electronic data sent out by a network to its affiliates. This is perhaps the point where *feed* officially made its way to the information age. Today, we enjoy the now ubiquitous *atom feed* or *RSS feed*—the preferred method by which we can receive our steady fix about a particular area of information—via the Internet as it becomes updated. In 2006, seven out of ten of the most statistically notable companions of *feed* have to do with information, not with food.

These days, it is possible that an RSS feed reaches us **wirelessly**. The latter is a word that first appeared in English just before the turn of the 20th century, to describe the transmission of a message. The adverb thereafter never achieved even a modicum of frequency, owing to a lack of applications. The related noun *wireless* on the other hand, which still retains a note of nostalgia, was somewhat more frequent, owing to its use to designate a radio receiver. Neither *wireless* nor *wirelessly*, however, occur at all in the Brown Corpus, one of the small but pioneering collections of language that was put together, mostly from American sources, in the 1960s.

Today, we don't need a corpus to know that *wireless* and *wirelessly* figure large in the discourse of almost every computer-literate generation. The Oxford corpus does, however, give us some interesting insight into how far the words have come. Gone are the days when we listened to programmes on the wireless. Here are the days when we discuss *broadband wireless access suppliers*. Most of the top companions (known by linguists as 'collocates') of *wireless* today are themselves new words that have only come to prominence in the 21st century: **broadband**, **Bluetooth**, **8021.1b**, **next-generation**. As for *wirelessly*, its prime collocates suggest that you have to be fully conversant with current technology even to use the word: they include **54 Mbps**, **Freescale**, **UWB**, **Wi-Fi**.

A number of other English words with strong credentials in traditional areas of discourse have acquired new meanings connected with information technology, and the signs are that these new meanings significantly outnumber the old. A further example of such dramatic shifts can be seen in the behaviour of the noun **attachment**. In the year 2000, the most likely word to come before it, overwhelmingly, was *emotional*. Some way down the list in the same year, with about a quarter as many hits, was *email*. In 2005–06 however, *emotional* was edged out by the new electronic kind of attachment, by a margin of about 20%. While this is unlikely to mean that we are giving up our emotional attachments in favour of email ones—probably not, as English is still quite big enough to accommodate both—it seems indisputable that we are now spending a lot more time writing and talking about our email attachments than about our emotional ones.

A similar, and perhaps slightly less alarming, trend can be seen with the noun **client**, a word that has enjoyed many meanings from its first appearance in English. Until the late 20th century, however, you could be fairly certain that when *client* was mentioned, the subject was either a person or an organization consisting of people.

ooth next-generation **broadband** Bluetooth **next-genera**

This is far from the case today. Judging by the corpus evidence of the company that the word keeps in current English, a *client* is very likely to be the machine that feeds us a steady stream of information: namely, a computer. Thus far in the 21st century, *client*'s main job seems to be to pick up more and more modifiers which relate to information technology: its companions are almost all high-tech: *P2P, wireless, built-in, FTP, AFS, email, VPN, ipsec, groupware, Linux, VOIP, Java.*

The torrent of information that characterizes life in the 21st century flows against a background in which another subject looms large in people's discourse: security, terrorism, and the constant threat of inexplicable violence. 11 September 2001 marked a sea change in the usage and frequency of a number of words that we use to talk about our security and the things that threaten it. The Oxford English Corpus is again instructive in pointing up the way that our use of these terms has evolved from that signal calendar date.

The word **terrorism** has understandably increased manyfold in terms of actual frequency in the public discourse since 2001, but the company it keeps has also changed. It is the object of a conflicting set of verbs these days: *condemn, prevent, combat,* and *fight* on the one hand, *condone, glorify, justify, incite,* and *support* on the other. Also markedly changed today, in contrast to usage at the turn of the century, is the frequent collocation of words connected with Islam in relation to terrorism: today, *Islamic, Islamist, Jihad, Jihadi,* and *Muslim* all figure prominently.

Other words not far removed from the subject of terrorism show patterns of increase since the turn of the century. The picture of **detainee** is somewhat disturbing: it is most typically the object of *torture, abuse, hold,* and *mistreat.* Only the word *release* in the list of top collocates suggests that a detainee is entitled to any hope. **Combatant** also shows a steady increase in usage, particularly since the introduction of the term *unlawful combatant* (a substitute for *prisoner of war* and as such not covered by the Geneva Convention) for detainees in Guantanamo Bay. Similarly, the peculiar status known in the US as *enemy combatant* first appears with moderate frequency in 2001. By 2007, fewer than one in ten combatants is of a kind other than the enemy.

It is probably inevitable that these two preoccupations of modern times—information itself and security—should influence each other, and so they do: there is ample evidence in the English of the 21st century that we are quite concerned with information about our security, and the security of our information. In fact, **information security** is a frequent collocation these days that was hardly on the radar screen before the turn of the century. Another steady climber in US discourse today that was practically unknown only a few years ago is **endpoint security**: that is, security at the point of access to a database where it is vulnerable. This normally means at the point where ordinary people are able to access it. The steady rise of the term **identity theft** is part and parcel of the same phenomenon. At the turn of the century, the most frequent sort of scam was a *trade scam*. These days, scamming is all of a more personal, and usually electronic, nature: *phishing, lottery, email, telephone,* and *dialler* all keep frequent company with the noun **scam**.

Reflecting these same trends, English in the year 2000 shows no frequent pattern of the verb **compromise** being related to information, although *safety* and *security* do make the league tables in that year of things likely to be compromised. Six years on, *privacy, confidentiality,* and *identity* join the list.

The other, somewhat darker side of the interaction of these two modern themes is the sort of information we gather, examine, and exploit with regard to our security. In 2004, the British Information Commissioner Richard Thomas warned that we were 'sleepwalking into a surveillance society'. The Oxford English Corpus seems to bear out his view, at least linguistically. The noun **surveillance** is on the rise, and it keeps an increasingly complicated set of companions. In 2000, adjectives such as *warrantless*, *covert*, and *constant* were scarcely on the radar screen in the company of *surveillance*. Today, however, they are among its most typical companions. As an attributive noun, *surveillance* has added several frequent adjuncts, including *camera*, *equipment*, *tape*, *operation*, *system*, and *footage*. While these were not unknown in the year 2000 or before, they were simply not frequent enough to appear at the top of the *surveillance* league tables.

The verb **surveil** is now also becoming an unremarkable term in today's media reporting, particularly in the US. The verb, according to the latest evidence, is an American coinage of the late 19th century, a back-formation from *surveillance*. *Surveil* lived a somewhat shadowy life throughout most of the 20th century, showing up most frequently in law enforcement jargon. It seemed to enjoy a particular vogue in the 1970s with the FBI and its *surveilling agents*, but after that the term seemed to go to ground. Thus far into the 21st century, however, it has already increased threefold over its usage throughout the 1990s. **Monitor**, a near-synonym with a wider field of application, also shows increasing usage with the passing years since 2000. Today, and in contrast with only a few years ago, some of its companions imply secretiveness and covert behaviour: both *secretly* and *surreptitiously* are both present with *monitor* today frequently enough to appear in statistics.

The word **order** offers a further example of a word which, over the course of the last several years, may be in flux. As a noun, *order* has various meanings relating to our security and our relationship to information: The phrases *law and order*, *public order*, and *establish order*, for example, all have implications for our security, and a great number of documents issued by authorities go by the name of *order*. Today, it may be a discomforting sign that the verb most typically used before *order*, both at the turn of the 21st century and now, is *disobey*. It may or may not be significant that synonyms for *disobey*—that is, *breach* and *defy*—also seem to show up more frequently now than they did six years ago. The sorts of orders that courts and authorities are issuing—*restraining*, *back-to-work*, *winding-up*, *confiscation*, and so on—are fairly constant over the same period, though *gag* order is more prevalent today than it was formerly (an attempt to suppress information perhaps), and one other, *ASBO* (for *antisocial behaviour order*), is now highly common in British discourse, beginning in 2003 and showing no signs of reduced frequency.

The comforting aspect of *order* in its work as a verb is that ordering a *pizza* and ordering a *retrial* seem to be as important now as they were when we began this century. Providing slightly more food for thought are the following: ordering *evacuations* (and their companions, *orders to evacuate*) are rather more frequent today than they were a few years ago. *Execution* seems not to have moved this century as the sort of thing that authorities can order, but ordering a *wiretap* has moved up. Orders to *shoot* and *attack* also seem to be increasing.

In 2006, the release of the German film 'The Lives of Others' (*Das Leben der Anderen*) delivered a compelling and chilling account of the activities of the East German Stasi (secret police) in monitoring the activities of citizens, among them leading artists. The depiction of Cold War surveillance makes uncomfortable viewing, and the film was lauded as a remarkable study of human values in a Big Brother society. Twenty years on from the time the film depicts, and among those words which are occurring with increasing frequency in today's conversation and writing, are some telling indicators of what preoccupies us today, and they are not so different. Information and security may well be the defining linguistic influences of this opening decade, and perhaps beyond.

words in the spotlight

bully

At the beginning of April 2007, British newspapers reported on concerns from a teachers' union about the rise of **cyberbullying**: the targeting by pupils of teachers and other children through hostile and defamatory emails, text messages, websites, and other devices of cyberspace.

Cyber-, combined with a range of words to indicate activity involving computers, is a phenomenon of the second half of the 20th century, but *bully* is a great deal older. Its connotations are now wholly negative.

It was not always so, however. The word *bully* probably derives from the Dutch word 'boel', meaning 'lover'. In the 16th century, *bully* was a term of endearment and went on to denote a fine fellow, or a gallant. In Shakespeare's *Midsummer Night's Dream*, his fellow mechanicals refer to their lost comrade as 'sweet bully Bottom'. In *Henry V*, one of his followers says admiringly of the King, 'from my heartstring I love the lovely bully'. However, from the end of the 17th century the more familiar sense emerged. The *Oxford English Dictionary* provides the evidence to show a progression in the negative sense of *bully* from the simple meaning of a blustering braggart, to what we would recognize today: 'a tyrannical coward who makes himself a terror to the weak'. It is quite a way from Agincourt to the world of cyberbullying.

3

The Sound of Science

The effect of scientific language is often misunderstood. Most lay people consider it opaque, while some credit it with deliberate obfuscation. In fact, like any shorthand intended for a specific community (and much like slang), the language of science is eminently clear and accessible to those immersed in the field under discussion. In scientific papers, everything is laid out as clearly and explicitly as possible: each scientific term has a precise meaning, narrowly defined and carefully deployed. Failure to be explicit, after all, could cause lasting damage to a scientist's career. Scientific language may—just as slang and business jargon do—carry inherent assumptions about the knowledge of those being addressed, but unlike those other 'codes' the language is also complex, highly unintuitive, and takes many years to grasp. Once mastered, it has a very different purpose from concealment. The purpose of scientific language is clarity.

It is when scientific terms are brought into the mainstream by non-scientists that rather different motives may be at work. Science adds authority, and the impulse to adopt the scientist's voice is strongly apparent in marketing and product packaging. Take the well-known strapline adopted by the Italian white goods manufac-turer Zanussi—**The Appliance of Science**, first introduced in the 1980s and still remembered today, or Audi's **Vorsprung durch**

Technik (which has the dual meaning of 'advancement through technology' and 'technologically one step ahead'). The latter tempts through the very idea of science: the specifics are passed over, just as long as we can be reassured that 'science' is there. In fact, if scrutiny wins over acceptance, it becomes evident that when technical language is appropriated for marketing, the result is often a blurring, and in some cases even a distortion, of the science behind it. Indeed this may be the most common fate of words that leave the laboratory and enter the vernacular.

A good example of a word absorbed into the mainstream in this diffuse way is **chemical**. In science, a 'chemical' is two or more atoms joined together by a chemical bond. They can be very simple, such as water or carbon dioxide, or enormously complex, as with proteins that contain many thousands of atoms and perform the essential functions of life. With very few exceptions, everything we eat, breathe, and use is made of chemicals. Over the past few years, however, it has become common to see products marketed as **chemical-free**—something which in scientific terms is fairly nonsensical. These 'non-chemicals' are often personal hygiene products such as deodorants and shampoos, or household cleaners, promoted as being less environmentally harmful. 'Chemical-free' is intended to communicate that they do not contain powerful, often synthetic and potentially hazardous ingredients. 'Chemical' has become synonymous with man-made, unnatural, and dangerous; even more so with the frequently iterated threat of **chemical weaponry** in the hands of terrorist states.

One multi-billion-dollar industry that has had a long-standing, complex relationship with scientific assertions is that of cosmetics. It is understandable that the purveyors of beauty products should wish to invoke science in order to convince. One popular claim is that a face cream will contain important-sounding **AHA** (**alpha hydroxy**) **acids** or **polyphenols**, both of which, however, are naturally occurring substances. Some companies seem to rely on happy confusion, as in the treatment 'Rest-a-Line', which is presumably intended to evoke Restylane, a 'filler' that dermatologists inject into the skin in order to flatten out wrinkles. Other products hint at working like **Botox**—the ultimate and explicit appliance of science—with names like Avotox, Serutox, and even Faux-Tox. The success of Botox is linguistically curious: the wholly negative idea of **toxins**, so closely associated with another modern phenomenon, **detoxing**, has with Botox been completely subsumed by the promise of a wrinkle-free complexion. The result is that poison is clearly invoked in one area, and lost in another.

As with Zanussi, 'science' within the cosmetics industry seems often to be wafted around as atmosphere, so that one company has as its current strapline 'Firmology: the science of sexy skin' (recalling the 80s ads for British Telecom in which a grandmother, played by Maureen Lipman, declares on hearing her grandson's exam results 'You've got an –ology!'). Another cosmetics line, drawing on medical imagery, invites the customer to '**Inject** Your Lashes with Volume'. 'Inject' here is being used the same way that it is in a phrase such as 'inject a little zip into your love life', and yet on the cosmetic pot or bottle, 'injecting' subtly invokes the syringe. A third sells eyeshadow in a form that requires two components to be mixed. The text, which advertises this product as 'bi-phase liquid eyeshadow', requires the user who wants blue eyelids to 'shake to mix 2 phases', a strangely technical use of the latter word.

The average western shopper at a cosmetics counter is likely to take most of the impressive language used with a pinch of salt. We are accommodated to the idea that while **slap** (a term which goes back to the 1860s and was first used in the theatre as a synonym for 'rouge') or **war paint** (also the 1860s) does its job in a straightforward manner, the semi-medical sounding anti-ageing cosmetic cream may not have profound effects. There are historical parallels in medicine too. The word **mountebank**, defined by the *Oxford English Dictionary* as 'an itinerant charlatan who sold supposed medicines and remedies, often using various entertainments to attract a crowd of potential customers', dates back to the 16th century. The word **quack** itself, almost as old, is defined as 'an ignorant pretender to medical or surgical skill; one who boasts to have a knowledge of wonderful remedies'. Going back centuries, that is, we are accustomed to being half-deceived by potions that sound too good to be true. However, a new trend in the cosmetics industry is beginning to suggest otherwise.

The word **cosmeceutical** is first recorded as a noun in 1985, and as an adjective in 1988, and is just now slipping out of the laboratory and into the press, to be tested out for usefulness by the public at large. 'Cosmeceutical' is a blend word, combining 'cosmetic' and 'pharmaceutical'. In law, the two are distinct. A cosmetic has a superficial, temporary effect, while a pharmaceutically active product, a medicine or drug, can actually alter a person. This difference is crucial, because anything classed as a medicine has to go through lengthy, complex, and expensive testing procedures to gain the licence that allows it to be sold. The regulatory standards for cosmetics are, by comparison, more liberal.

As scientific research reaches new heights in the area of the dream product, a cream that will genuinely reverse the effects of ageing on skin, the term 'cosmeceutical' has become necessary to cover products that, contrary to jaded expectations, have a non-cosmetic effect. There are available now, for example, creams that slightly alter the skin's underlying dermis (structurally plumping out wrinkles), and which promise 'instant illuminating radiance', 'visibly young firmness', or to 'reveal younger-looking skin'. We take today such claims as read, but when one leading British chemist produced in 2007 a beauty **serum** (containing a unique **antioxidant** complex with added skin-firming **pro-retinol**) with scientifically proven effects documented in a BBC2 documentary series, the effect was astounding. Over the ensuing weeks supplies proved impossible to maintain and waiting lists were set up, with purchases limited to one per applicant. The BBC's mass mobiliza-tion of avid purchasers demonstrates the extent of the public's capacity for trusting to science when mediated in what seemed like a plausible manner. Yet by the same token, it may perhaps indicate that scientific language, as commonly deployed on such products, has in fact long lost its clarity—the very opposite result to what it set out to achieve.

auty serum **antioxidant** pro-retinol **beauty serum** antioxi

words in the spotlight

granularity

Metaphors linking information with food and consumption are certainly not new: the noteworthy aspect about them today is their unstoppable increase. An article in 2007 in the *Washington Post* decried the use of the term **granularity** as a new buzzword for 'specificity' on the grounds that it was a scientific and technical word encroaching on popular usage.

The *Post*'s observation was an accurate one: in 2007 the top US commander in Iraq, responding to the question as to whether sectarian violence in the country would increase after US troops withdraw, said: 'It's hard from this distance... to get a real feel, or the real granularity of what's going on.' He was far from alone in his use of the term. The White House Secretary Tony Snow, speaking of the difficulty in establishing a connection between Saddam Hussein and Abu Musab al-Zarqawi, stated that 'we just don't have that kind of granularity in terms of the relationship'.

'Granularity' is now a buzzword used to mean 'detail' or, as the *Washington Post* article put it, 'the nitty gritty'. In a longer view, the word is simply a further iteration of the abstraction of a food term that has finally made its way to information (see the discussion of 'feed' in 'Bigger Brother', pp 29–38).

After its initial coinage in the late 1800s as an extension of 'grain', a seed, the term found various applications in cell biology. In its current sense it began as a reference to the number of pixels in a computer graphic, which determines the depth of detail in the image. One suggestion as to why we now need 'granularity' to talk about information is that we now regard that information as a uniform and plentiful substance for consumption. Its nutritive value is determined by the degree to which we can ascertain its individual ingredients.

Today, 'granularity' is applied to everything from the proposal for a new baseball stadium to a situation as serious as that in Iraq. It is quite definitely a buzzword of the moment.

4

Us and Them:
The Language of Division

Mate, Are you extracting the Michael? Me and my bezzies from the glossy posse, like, literally died when we asked Daddy to read us your article 'Just don't say Yah...'. Like, you even got the meaning of birdage wrong. Birdage is when your bezzer like properly redges you to chat with some totty.

A Letter to the Editor in the *Times*, January 2007, responding to an article announcing the return of the Sloane Ranger.

Pedigree v Pit Bull: Big Brother's cynical face

The Times, January 2007, header to a report on the hostility on *Celebrity Big Brother* between Shilpa Shetty and Jade Goody.

New words are rarely predictable. They can be the result of a moment's creativity or, more probably, the answer to an immediate need for a name to describe a new technological, cultural, or social phenomenon. The sources of neologisms however, particularly over a period of time, often *can* be anticipated. Online technology is just one example of an area that has been a key and consistent generator of new vocabulary and of language change in the 21st century. In the same period, however, there has been one notable catalyst for word-coining which few at the beginning of the century

would have foretold. Social labelling, and the heightened awareness of class that it reflects, has produced a new lexicon of tribal
vocabulary which suggests very strongly that society, far from
becoming more democratic, is polarizing itself into a situation
of 'us and them'.

The most obvious and widely discussed of the new social labels to
emerge in this opening decade was **chav** (see 'The Winners and
the Losers', pp 8–28). Coined some hundred and fifty years ago, so
linguists believe, this Romany word for an unmarried Romany man
or male child was given a new and sinister twist in 2004 when it
came to be used to describe everything from an individual to an
entire social class, of which the *Daily Mail* declared: 'They're white,
they're dumb, they're vulgar.'

'Chav' joined a fairly long list of others of the same kind. **Skangers**,
spides, **charvers**, and **neds** are Scottish, Irish, Northern English,
and Northern Irish labels respectively for people with the same
alleged characteristics—in other words uneducated, lower-class,
and vulgarly dressed. **Pikey** became another controversial term for
someone considered to be a lout, having started out as a derogatory
term for a Gypsy (a now recognized distinct ethnic group). In 2005,
Steve Lowe and Alan McArthur in a best-selling book entitled 'Is It
Me or Is Everything Shit?' gave the new trend in class mockery the
name **Nu-snobbery**—the belief, in other words, that 'the poor are
a right laugh'.

The ridicule of others perceived to be of a lower social order is of
course nothing new. It stretches back to Victorian times and
beyond. In 1785, Grose's *Dictionary of the Vulgar Tongue* included
the entry **Whitechapel** as the name of a new social breed, defining
those within it as 'fat, ragged, and saucy'. The energy with which

ers **chav** skangers **spides** Nu-snobbery **Hooray Henries** social mockery (which also works upwards—hence **Hooray Henries**, **Sloane Rangers**, and **yahs**) has resurfaced in the 21st century is however a surprise—as are, in some quarters at least, those who appear to espouse it. In the spring of 2006 Prince William was reported to have dressed up in a white baseball cap, a sweatshirt, and flashy jewellery to celebrate the completion of his first term at the military academy Sandhurst. The *Sun* declared that the Prince was now the 'Future bling of England', having been challenged to 'put on a chavvy accent and stop speaking like a Royal'.

On television, too, class distinctions were a popular source of comedy. Once again the trend was already there, but while previous comedy heroes such as Del Boy (*Only Fools and Horses*) and Fletcher (*Porridge*) were both objects of affection, today's Vicky Pollard (from *Little Britain*), whose couldn't-care-less attitude is crystallized in her 'wha'ev-ah' catchphrase, was noticeably different. Even the name **Vicky** came to be used as shorthand for those girls sporting **council house facelifts** (hair drawn tightly into a bun) at society's bottom end.

Beyond the labels coined for the new social types, it was their fashion and tastes (or perceived lack of them) which provoked language change—**hoodies**, **prison-whites** (brand new trainers often discarded once worn), **flash trash**, and **pimp gold** were among the main objects of derision. Such was the criticism levelled at those sporting such wardrobes that support came from surprising quarters—the leader of the Conservative Party David Cameron declared in 2006 that it was time to empathize with the wearers of hooded sweatshirts. Rather than banning them from shopping malls in a pre-emptive strike against antisocial behaviour, the British public should, Cameron declared, examine its conscience.

flash trash pimp gold hoodies Nu-snobbery Hooray Henri

That he never actually spoke the catchphrase subsequently taken up by the media was irrelevant: **hug a hoodie** encapsulated the new liberal face of the right.

For many, the phenomenon of the 'chav' was a new kind of social racism. While it was one of the most dramatic representations of a sea change in social intolerance, however, it was far from the only example of the 'us and them' mentality. The 2000s provided many instances where the choice of a single word to categorize an entire group of people had quite dramatic consequences.

The 2007 series of the reality TV show *Celebrity Big Brother* attracted an unprecedented number of complaints to the UK broadcasting watchdog Ofcom. Their catalyst was the treatment of the Indian actress and model Shilpa Shetty by fellow contestants including Jade Goody, a former *Big Brother* contestant herself, and her family. This treatment was perceived to be bullying and racist, sparking widespread condemnation in the media and mass demonstrations in India. Back in the *Big Brother* house, Shetty was allegedly given the name 'Shilpa Poppadom', while certain of her fellow inmates expressed the wish that she would 'go home'. In a vivid illustration of how racism dominates the modern list of taboos, a Channel 4 spokesman reassured viewers that in one particular outburst, when an offensive word was bleeped out by the broadcasters, it was in fact 'the c-word' that had been used against Shetty, rather than 'Paki'.

If c*** was clearly considered by TV bosses to be a word less offensive and worthy of condemnation, the *Sun* decided to draw from the episode a lesson in equality. The day after Shilpa Shetty emerged as the winner of the series, the paper showed on its front page a group of children each holding up board signs as identity markers. On them were written tags such as **yid**, **spic**, **chavscum**, **towel head**, **rag head**, **pikey**, **half-breed**, **terrorist**, and **nigger**. The headline presented the children's question as 'What do we have in common?' The answer, given on the following page, was: 'We're all British.'

Programmes such as *Big Brother* have, in the view of some, had a major hand in the re-emergence of class consciousness. Jade Goody herself was mocked for her lack of sophistication and education during her first appearances on the show. Jim Shelley, writing in the *Mirror* in the aftermath of the Shetty vs Goody furore, commented 'in her first series, Jade was paraded like something from the circus —a bona fide live chav for us all to gawp at. This year it's as if they've brought in a "genuine family of pikeys—never before seen on TV!"'

The lack of social graces ascribed to Jade Goody came once more to the fore when a Buckingham Palace spokesman announced in April 2007 that Prince William and his girlfriend Kate Middleton were to split. The inevitable media speculation reached fever pitch when one royal commentator speculated that the real reason for the break-up was Kate Middleton's mother, a former flight attendant whose background may have been considered to be socially inferior and who had reputedly said on meeting the Queen 'Pleased to meet you' instead of the preferred 'How do you do?' (in fact, there appeared to be real doubt as to whether the Queen had actually ever met Carole Middleton). In the course of the subsequent debate the words **U** and **non-U** were resurrected to denote social accept-ability. The concepts of 'upper-class' and 'non-upper-class' and their reflection in language were the subject of a study by the philologist Alan Ross and popularized by the novelist Nancy Mitford in her tongue-in-cheek work *Noblesse Oblige* in 1956. In the latter, Mitford provided a glossary of terms considered 'U', which included 'napkin' (not 'serviette'), 'looking glass' (not 'mirror'), and 'cycle' (not 'bike'). Carole Middleton's reported preference for 'toilet' rather than 'lavatory' had distinct echoes of George Bernard Shaw's *Pygmalion* from almost a century earlier. Here, as in the play, linguistic choices were perceived as the final arbiter in judging suitability for the higher classes.

2007 provided many more instances of the use of the wrong word in the wrong context, most of which were far more highly charged than those attributed to Mrs Middleton. In the summer of 2006 the Virginia Senator George Allen was forced to apologize for what his opponent considered to be insensitive and demeaning remarks to a volunteer of Indian descent at a campaign rally. In his speech, Allen had pointed at the man and remarked: 'This fellow here, over here with the yellow shirt, macaca, or whatever his name is. He's with my opponent. He's following us around everywhere… Let's give a welcome to macaca, here. Welcome to America and the real world of Virginia.' **Macaca**, depending on how it is spelled, can mean a monkey (usually spelled 'macaque') that inhabits the Eastern hemisphere, or a town in South Africa. In some European cultures it is considered to be a distinct racial slur against African immigrants. Allen denied that he knew the true meaning of the word. Whether or not his remark was intended to be offensive, **macaca moment** entered the political lexicon as a linguistic faux pas with potentially disastrous results.

A similar error of judgement was made by the Massachusetts governor Mitt Romney, who referred to Boston's troubled highway commuter tunnel project as a **tar baby**. Black leaders were outraged by his use of a term which dates back to the 19th century and the 'Uncle Remus' stories before being taken up as a derogatory term for a black person as well as a more neutral term for a sticky problem. Governor Romney insisted he referred only to the latter meaning. Far more damagingly, the US 'shock jock' Don Imus was dismissed from his job after calling the members of the Rutgers University's women's basketball team a bunch of **nappy-headed hos**. For Imus, the use of words accepted in one place caused trouble in another—**ho**, short for 'whore', is a word much used by rappers. In the wake of Imus's comments, the MC Snoop Dogg defended the use of the word in rap lyrics as entirely different, namely for 'ho's that's in the hood that ain't doing shit, that's trying to get a nigga for his money. These are two separate things.' Def Jam co-founder Russell Simmons thought differently and called for a voluntary ban by rappers on the terms **ho**, **bitch**, and **nigger**. Meanwhile Mr Imus's defenders ventured that he was actually an equal-opportunity offender and that Jews, gays, and Roman Catholics were also his frequent targets. Their efforts failed to save his job.

National characteristics have long been the subject of stereotype. In a final example of the entrenchment of an 'us and them' mentality, an Australian beer ad which depicted Englishmen as perpetual moaners was pulled after a group of English campaigners complained. The radio ad for 'Toohey's New Supercold beer' showed a group of Englishmen singing to the tune of 'Land of Hope and Glory' using various synonyms for grumbling, including 'whine', 'moan', 'slag off', and 'complain'. The Australian Advertising Standards Bureau ruled that such a presentation negatively stereotyped the British.

The use of language to differentiate ourselves from others and to reinforce a perceived sense of superiority has taken many new forms in the course of the new century. Tribal branding is not just

let macaca moment **tar baby** British moaners **ho** bitch t self-selected, as is the case with the slang used by groups who set themselves apart with their choice of words. It can equally be a form of attack, as potent as any racial or ethnic slur. Public reaction to each of the episodes above provides a strong marker as to our changing taboos, where social labels are in some cases holding sway over those related to ethnicity. Whether or not a backlash comes soon is hard to predict. Perhaps the one thing we can say with certainty is that it will be language which will be the first and strongest indicator of change.

words in the spotlight

Maafa

At the end of March 2007, a ceremony in Westminster Abbey to commemorate the 200-year anniversary of the parliamentary abolition of the slave trade was interrupted by a protester calling on the representatives of Church and State to apologize for Britain's role in the **Maafa**. In his view, the ceremony—which marked the culmination of efforts in the late 18th and early 19th centuries by the Abolitionist William Wilberforce and his supporters—was a 'Wilberfest' or 'Wilberfarce' which ignored both the terrible reality of the slave trade, and the lasting guilt incurred.

Maafa is a Swahili word which means 'unspeakable horror'. Since the 1990s, it has increasingly been used among those of African descent as an alternative to 'Black Holocaust', itself a term which draws an explicit parallel between what was done to the Jewish people in the 20th century and what was done to Africans during the long reign of the slave trade. This choice of a significant name to mark an episode of particular horror echoes the adoption in the mid 20th century of the Hebrew word *shoah*—'catastrophe'—as a preferred term for what was more generally described as the 'Holocaust'.

Whether or not it will fully replace 'Holocaust', *Shoah* has become a widely understood term. With increasing attention focused on the history of the 'African Diaspora', it seems likely that *Maafa* may well in turn become part of the general vocabulary.

5

Minds, Hearts, and Coronets:
Political Language

In the political arena, the linguistic evidence from the 21st century is strongly suggestive of the ebb and flow of power. While internationally the political graph saw quite tumultuous rises in the emotional temperature of both the public and the politicians, prompted by war and its aftermath, it reached at home in 2006–7 an uneasy flat line which characterized the approach of the end of office. As Tony Blair and George Bush began their last periods of political leadership, the nations they presided over hovered in a state of political limbo. The language of the last six years has been powerfully indicative of the shifting patterns of power. In both the US and the UK, the language of the successful, expansionist election winner gave way to a far more cautious vocabulary as the end of leadership grew closer.

In Britain, it was the question of the Prime Minister's successor—the neatly dubbed **Blair Switch Project**—which dominated debate in the House of Commons. More specifically, at least for many months before any official announcement was made, the preoccupation was with precisely when the handover would take place. Months of speculation followed Tony Blair's confirmation that he would not be fighting a fourth election and would cede leadership sometime during the next political term. The *Observer*'s William

Keegan put it thus in March 2007: 'Although the Church …has abolished limbo, Britain and New Labour have not.'

The rivalry between Tony Blair and his successor, Gordon Brown, was a constant theme not just in the approach to the PM's stepping down, but for almost his entire leadership. The so-called **Granita Pact** referred to an alleged deal between Brown and Blair, made at an Islington eaterie, that Brown would give Blair a clear run for the Labour Party leadership on the understanding that Blair would eventually stand down and make way for him. The perceived refusal of Blair to keep his side of the bargain when he stood for a third term as party leader led to media reporting of bitter feuding backstage: Labour, it was said, was having an attack of the **Teebee Geebees** (i.e. the TB/GBs). As the anticipation of Blair's stepping down grew more feverish, the inevitability of a smooth and unchallenged succession by the Chancellor looked shaken amid talk of an **ABG** camp. 'ABG', or Anyone but Gordon, was a successor to the **ABC** campaign of the early Bush years: the 'C' referring to Bill Clinton. For Brown, the allegiance from some fellow cabinet members was not in doubt; others, including John Reid, took some time before they declared their hand. Newspapers naturally joined in the speculation: one *Scotland on Sunday* headline declared 'Reid in the wind is bound to end up a Brownie'. Brown's supporters were also referred to as Brownites and, inevitably, Brownistas.

Among many images used to describe Tony Blair's position in his closing days in office, one in particular cropped up frequently: that of being **in the bunker**. Even the word **frit**, famously popularized by Margaret Thatcher for one of her lily-livered opponents, began to be resurrected by journalists as a term for those who occupied political seats. The choice was an interesting one, and reflected a general and significant shift in political language on both sides of the Atlantic over the course of the new century.

Britain in the 1990s was characterized by a supreme sense of confidence. **Cool Britannia** was in a mood of celebration, and political speech was punctuated by the words **New**, **enterprise**, and **trust**. The dominance of the political leader was indisputable: indeed, the phrase **what Tony wants** was used by critics to characterize the new style of government, in which directors of communication (or, in the opinion of others, orchestrators of **spin**) assumed a more important, vocal, and explicit role than many could remember. The new imperative was to be **on message** as the leader's rule became all-conquering. Such confidence was echoed in the language of the opening months of the new Bush administration in 2001: according to an article entitled 'Confidence Men' in *Washington Monthly* in reference to the President's 'talk, bluff, and bluster', 'the confidence man's utter self-assurance can sometimes become a self-fulfilling prophecy. Like a savvy card player he can bluff his opponents out of the game without even holding a decent hand.'

Six years on, the language of leadership in 2007 reflected a new insecurity, betrayed in the choice of both leaders' choice of expression and an inevitable offshoot perhaps of political limbo. The bullishness of **spin** and **prebuttal**, of **slash-and burn politics** (an in'eresting metaphor, borrowed from agriculture where virgin forests are cut down and burnt prior to the planting of seeds, and denoting a highly aggressive, swingeing form of politics) was replaced by the backfoot language of **slime and defend** policies (whereby a party under attack defends itself by slandering its opposition), and by far more conservative terms such as Gordon Brown's **progressive consensus**. Days before Tony Blair's departure, the

in **Cool Britannia** spin **prebuttal** slash-and-burn **war on**

Leader of the Opposition was making reference to the **government of the living dead**.

Nowhere was a shift in tone more apparent than in communications about the ongoing conflict in Iraq and the daily reports of multiple killings, both military and civilian. Here the fighting talk of earlier years was markedly lacking. In many cases the choice of wording was considered and deliberate, as politicians were reminded of the power of language. This not only entailed the adoption of conciliatory and rationalizing vocabulary, but also the abandonment of some phrases which had previously been key features of pro-war rhetoric. In April 2007 it emerged that Labour were quietly dropping the term **war on terror**. Hilary Benn, Labour Minister for International Development, rationalized it thus: 'In the UK, we do not use the phrase "war on terror" because we can't win by military means alone, and because this isn't us against one organized enemy with a clear identity and a coherent set of objectives.' Nor was it felt that the term threatened that enemy: on the contrary, it could be harnessed to their own propaganda, a point made many years earlier by Margaret Thatcher who believed any terrorist's cause should be 'starved …from the oxygen of publicity'. The term 'war on terror' had in fact long been in dispute, with critics arguing that 'war' suggested a clear resolution at its end, something which was proving notably elusive in Iraq.

Other terms had already faded from view: **axis of evil** and **moral crusade**, both central to the Bush administration's heavily religious rhetoric at the beginning of the war, were succeeded by the more tempered **moral case for intervention**, the invocation of **fairness**, and the apologetic tones of following **instinct**. In early 2007 it was announced that the Bush administration was abandoning the phrase **stay the course** when speaking of the war, as part of an effort to emphasize US flexibility in the face of some of the bloodiest violence since the beginning of the conflict. 'He stopped using it,' stated the White House press secretary. 'It left the wrong impression about what was going on', while the President himself stated: 'Stay the course means keep doing what you're doing. My attitude is, don't do what you're doing if it's not working; change.'

Hearts and minds was a phrase which fared rather better; it still features regularly in the political expression of the imperative to gain confidence and cooperation from the electorate. A phrase from the Bible's Philippians, it was also much used by the US military in Vietnam in a campaign to win the popular support of the Vietnamese people. Often chosen to signify at best a misguided, and at worst a propagandist, attempt to justify war and to persuade the people of an invaded country that they will be better off, it was thus rather surprising that it was used in Congress and the House of Commons at the beginning of the 2003 war in Iraq. Its history and double-edged interpretation seem not to have deterred politicians from regular use even today.

The emotional appeal of 'hearts and minds' resonates with an intimacy which has very much characterized political speech over the past five years. The direct conversational approach of the British PM, whose verbal habits of 'y'know' and 'frankly' encapsulated the whole idea of Labour's **Big Conversation** with its electors, was part of the party's **New Emotionalism** which seemed to drive its language as much as its political priorities. This kind of direct appeal and informal tone was matched by campaign slogans from its rival Conservative party such as (in 2005) 'I mean, how hard is it to keep a hospital clean?' In 2006 in a speech on social justice, the Conservative party leader David Cameron called for more understanding of young people who commit crime. The media and the

earts and minds **Big Conversation** New Emotionalism hea

Labour party leapt on his talk of 'hoodies': hooded sweatshirt-wearing teenagers who were in the process of being banned from many British shopping centres. The result, although never actually uttered by Cameron himself, was the sarcastic phrase **hug a hoodie**, used to lampoon the Conservative leader for his perceived naivety and soft-heartedness.

In 2007, it was Cameron again who propelled another phrase into the headlines, after launching a video aimed at provoking the young to political responsiveness. The video featured a young man tempted into overspending, in a story characterized by a battle between the young man's conscience and his **inner tosser**. It was the use of the surprisingly direct slang term 'tosser', which has its origins in a synonym for masturbation, which became the focus of debate, not—as the Conservatives would have wished—the aim to waken young voters from their apathy.

Such was the desire to make campaigning a more interactive process (evident on the other side of the Atlantic too, where Senator Hillary Clinton's bid to be a presidential candidate featured the word 'conversation' to represent her approach on her campaign trail), that **blogging** became a new force in political communication. David Cameron's own official **WebCameron** blog included a video of him washing the dishes at his family home while talking about cleaning up politics. Soon after, a spoof blog, the result of **cybersquatting** (the setting up of a rival website with a near identical web address), offered its own video parodying the leader's likeness to Tony Blair.

Reading a blog is often likened to listening to a conversation, albeit one written down. At a summit of the Group of Eight industrialized nations in the summer of 2006, it was an overheard and real conversation which hit the headlines. In this case, it was one clearly not intended for the public domain, and which was taken to reveal the real nature of the relationship between the US and the UK leaderships. '**Yo, Blair**. How are you doing?' seemed to be the folksy greeting that President Bush gave to Tony Blair during a pause in proceedings at the summit. The ensuing impromptu conversation, intended to be private, was picked up by a nearby microphone. Bush went on to discuss a recent flare-up in Lebanon between Israeli forces and the Shi'a group Hezbollah. 'What they need to do is get Syria to get Hezbollah to stop doing this shit.' 'Yo' quickly took hold in Britain. A cartoon by Gerald Scarfe in the *Sunday Times* showed George Bush dressed as a sheriff and seated in a rocking chair, saying to his Secretary of State Condoleezza Rice: 'Yo, Condi. Better go check out that sh*t. Don't hurry.' The satirical magazine *Private Eye* began its regular letter from the vicar of St Albion's fictional church with the greeting 'Yo', and the epistle included further variants, including 'Yo, Running Scared', and 'Yo, Dubya' (an established nickname for Bush based on his middle initial W).

If the spirit of apology has been a presence in the political discourse of recent years, the calls for politicians and religious leaders to express regret for major injustices committed (in many cases before their lifetime) have been loud and insistent. One of the very first things that Tony Blair did in office was to apologize for the indifference of 'those who governed in London' towards the Irish potato famine 150 years before. It represented the first apology expressed by the British authorities. As the calls for apologies for other tragedies multiplied, the language chosen by those in power attracted increasing scrutiny. The key distinction was whether their words expressed the desire to accept culpability and to make amends, or whether they stopped at present-day responsibilities and the need to ensure such injustices never recur. For those who demanded the first, the word **reparation** was central to their argument. In the US, slavery reparation—paid compensation to the descendants of those subjected to slavery—became a serious political issue and a real possibility.

In November 2006, on the eve of the bicentenary of the legislation of 1807 pioneered by William Wilberforce to abolish the slave trade, Blair stopped short of a full apology but expressed 'deep sorrow' for Britain's role in the slave trade. The debate over whether British and American leaders should apologize was heated and long (see **Maafa**, pp 54–5).

The call for apologies from politicians is of course not new, nor is it limited to injustices of history. In April 2007 the Secretary of State for Defence, Des Browne, said sorry before the House of Commons for sanctioning the sale, by a number of soldiers held hostage in Iran, of stories for significant sums of money. Many believed his apology to be grudging but necessary if resignation was to be avoided. A cartoon in the *Guardian*, by Steve Bell, showed Browne as Tony Blair's ventriloquist doll uttering the words 'I ngade a ngistake, a terrigle ngistake!'

The depiction of Des Browne as Tony Blair's puppet echoed a key theme in political imagery this century, namely that of acting and the theatre. The metaphor of the political stage is of course not new, but critics of the Labour government have found it a useful one in connection with perceived spin. In a *Guardian* article on Gordon Brown's last budget speech as Chancellor, Jonathan Freedland concluded that Brown had behaved as an **actor and showman**, and that he had obviously learned 'from the great thespian next door'. The description was not dissimilar to one often made of Harold Macmillan as **the old actor-manager**.

In fact, when it came to political imagery, Gordon Brown was a popular subject. As the likelihood of his accession to the leadership approached, he became the recipient of many allusive references. The Labour MP Frank Field likened Gordon Brown to Mrs Rochester, the madwoman who burns down her husband's mansion in Charlotte Brontë's novel *Jane Eyre*. 'Allowing Gordon Brown into No 10 would be like letting Mrs Rochester out of the attic,' he declared. The result was many jibes in the House of Commons from the Conservative benches. A few weeks later Lord Turnbull, Britain's former top civil servant, launched another, aggressive, attack on Gordon Brown, accusing him of having a **Stalinist** ruthlessness and a 'very cynical view of mankind and his colleagues'. In his budget speech Mr Brown deflected the Stalin jibe: 'May I thank for their hard work, and sometimes forthright advice, the civil servants—or should I say comrades?—who worked with me…'

These allusions served only to spawn others. In his column in the *Guardian* Simon Hoggart wrote: 'Gordon Brown isn't Stalin—he's New Labour's Robin Hood. He and his Gloomy Men sit under a tree. "I say, Robin, isn't our job to steal from the rich and give to the poor?" "No, that would not be prudent. We shall steal from everybody and then give everybody something back, on a fiscally neutral basis."' There was also much royal imagery around, especially in the use of **coronation**, again in reference to Brown whose automatic succession (as the **heir apparent**) was challenged by some. On Brown's eventual promotion to PM, the media talked of his being **anointed**. Simon Jenkins in the *Sunday Times* of March 2007 announced in his column, 'The king is about to die, long live the king, Gordon Brown', while Andrew Rawnsley in the *Observer* referred to the position of deputy leadership as 'the hollow privilege of being King Gordon's cupbearer'.

The idea of kingship looked set to stay, and was an interesting counterpart to the common description of Tony Blair's having made the role of Prime Minister **presidential**. Early on in his premiership, his then Director of Communications and Strategy Alastair Campbell deflected a question from a US journalist about Blair's religious beliefs with a flat 'We don't do God'. Many concluded in 2007 that Blair was to do just that following his departure from office, when he announced that one of his projects would be to establish an inter-faith foundation.

All of this evoked words from history attributed to Winston Churchill on being told that Clement Attlee had performed well as PM: 'If any grub is fed on Royal Jelly it turns into a Queen Bee.' When Blair embarked on a long series of international trips soon after he set the date for his departure, critics railed against a one-man **farewell tour**.

Euphemism has long featured large in political life. During the war in Iraq new examples emerged for the act of killing, including **deconflicting**, while **collateral damage** became the new term of choice for civilian casualties which resulted from military operations. **Blue on Blue** and **friendly fire** continued to designate the accidental killing of a member of one's own side or of an ally. The euphemism which attracted most attention, however, was **extraordinary rendition**. The term was probably coined by the CIA and referred to the transfer of prisoners to another country for interrogation. The extradition of a subject for interrogation to a country where that subject may be in danger is against American law, just as the application of torture to extract information from a suspect is against international law. It was widely assumed that movement to another country meant that the laws of the Geneva Convention would not apply, just as the term **unlawful combatants** for

Guantanamo Bay (**gitmo**) prisoners rather than 'prisoners of war' took the process outside the Convention's rules. Writing in January 2006, Salman Rushdie said of 'extraordinary rendition': 'Every so often the habitual newspeak of politics throws up a term whose calculated blandness makes us shiver with fear— yes, and loathing.'

Whether the political climate of 2007 was one of eager expectancy or limbo, the mood was clearly very different from that with which the century began. Throughout, language has articulated both the changes of the intervening years and their lack of conclusion. As Benjamin Disraeli put it, speaking of a much earlier time, 'Finality is not the language of politics.'

words in the spotlight

surge

At a press conference in December 2006, President Bush was questioned about the new Iraq strategy which he was to announce the following month. One possibility was an increase in the troops sent to Baghdad, but he noted that he wanted to gather all recommendations on this point. 'Then I'll report back to you as to whether or not I support a surge or not.'

Surge, recorded in English as a noun since the late medieval period, goes back ultimately to Latin *surgere* 'to rise'. Early uses are associated with the idea of a billow of water rising to a high point before falling back. From this came the modern extended sense of a rapid increase over a short period (as in a 'population surge'), not necessarily accompanied by a falling back to the original levels.

From the winter of 2006–7, 'the surge' was widely used to denote a possible increase in troop strength in Iraq. The implication of the term was that the increase would be a temporary one, rather than something that would need to be sustained over a long period. Some, however, were doubtful. Senator Edward Kennedy, speaking for the Democratic Party, said in early January that 'an escalation, whether it is called a surge or any other name, is still an escalation'. He added ominously, with reference to an earlier conflict: 'The Department of Defense kept assuring us that each new escalation in Vietnam would be the last. Instead, each one led only to the next.'

'Escalation' was a term particularly associated with the war in Vietnam. As appears to be happening with 'surge', the term itself began to be used as a kind of shorthand for the policy with which it was linked.

There are other precedents. During the First World War, many strategists thought that the equivalent of a surge was what was needed to break the deadlock. The *Times* of 10 July 1916 reported an interview given by Lord Derby, then Under Secretary for War, to the *Brooklyn Eagle*. Asked 'whether he believed the present British offensive to be the "big push"', he replied that 'Anything which decimates the German Army is a "big push". I do not believe it possible to characterize any given military operation as the final offensive. The task of defeating Germany is a slow task.'

Given that they were on the brink of the Battle of the Somme, with two more years of war ahead, Derby's caution was understandable, but it is also clear that the 'big push' had taken on a life of its own in the public mind. In July of that year, the *Times* published a column of interviews with survivors from the Somme. One of them was quoted as saying: 'I want to get back and see this big push out.'

In the end, neither 'the big push', nor indeed 'escalation', has been associated with lasting military or political success. Linguistically, however, they have all established themselves as key terms for a particular period and engagement. In 2007, it remains to be seen how 'surge' will be remembered.

6

'Ding Dong':
The Shorthand of Catchphrases

Like any good catchphrase, in order to be truly successful 'Ya Burnt!' will require heavy use by the Gen X, Y and Nexters. However, I believe strongly that it is so potentially sophisticated Boomers will be using it in divorce proceedings, book club arguments and sex therapy.

> A blogger writing in the group weblog and news site *The Huffington Post*, March 2007.

In March 2007, reports of the death of the actor John Inman were accompanied by references to his most famous role, as the camp 'Mr Humphries' in the long-running sitcom *Are You Being Served?* (1972–85). It was clear from the coverage that the Inman/Humphries creation was defined by his catchphrase 'I'm free!', one which worked both on the literal level as the natural response of a sales assistant in the Grace Brothers' emporium, and as an acceptable (for the time) covert allusion to a gay identity.

The most linguistically successful catchphrases typify a particular individual. The February 2007 issue of *The Oldie* carried an interview with the veteran actor Leslie Phillips headed 'Behind the catchphrase'. The article referred not only to his 'trademark comic lecherous catchphrase "Hello!"', but to other expressions like

'Lumme' and 'Ding dong'. Phillips was quoted as saying, 'Even today, I am regularly ding-donged as I walk around London'— evidence, as the interviewer commented, that his identity with these catchphrases had fixed him in the public mind as a kind of comic English stereotype of the 1950s and 1960s.

A catchphrase can become part of the general vocabulary very quickly. The 'Am I bovvered?' of Catherine Tate's stroppy teenager Lauren is always used in the confidence that it will be recognized. In March 2007, Comic Relief's Red Nose Day telethon featured a sketch in which Lauren undertook work experience at 10 Downing Street. Tony Blair commented afterwards that 'Meeting Lauren was an experience. She didn't seem "bovvered" by anything.'

A week later, Gordon Brown presented a budget offering a tax cut— which for some commentators wrong-footed the Conservatives. The columnist Matthew Norman, writing in the *Independent* of 23 March about the Tory leader David Cameron, found Lauren a useful reference point: 'After Wednesday, it will be a while before he feels tempted to ape the Prime Minister by posing the rhetorical quest-ion, "Am I bovvered?" Bovvered to the point of raw panic is what the Tory leader should be today.'

In 2003, the comedy historian Robert Ross put 'I'm free' at the top of his list of 20 classic sitcom catchphrases. It was followed by Basil Fawlty's 'Don't mention the war', and Victor Meldrew's 'I don't *believe* it!' These however were all catchphrases which had had time to establish themselves in the language. It is just as interesting to look at some of the new contenders coming into the frame.

In March 2007, a blog on the *Huffington Post* discussed a catch-phrase from the new NBC comedy *30 Rock*: the exclamation 'Ya

Don't mention the war I don't believe it! Ding Dong He

Burnt!' used as a silencing riposte. In the blogger's view, 'Ya Burnt' was 'poised to take the lead in American catchphrases', the equivalent to the 90s phrase 'In your face!'.

Meanwhile the Avon company, revealing its new 'Hello Tomorrow' slogan in 2007, was said to be trying to move away from what, in its time, had been a hugely successful campaign catchphrase. Avon cosmetics are famously sold by 'Avon Ladies', and from the 1950s the line 'Ding Dong—Avon calling!' came to personify the brand. References by the media to 'the ding-dong era' underlined the success of the original slogan: linguistically, an allusion to it can now conjure up the world of the 1970s. It also provides an example of the importance of context: Avon's 'ding dong' comes from the same time as that of Leslie Phillips, but otherwise it is a world away.

Every period has its catchphrases. One hundred years ago, in 1907, the phrase of the moment was the triumphant 'Meredith, we're in!', from a music-hall sketch *The Bailiff*. It seems unlikely that this would evoke many echoes today, but it had an impressively long run. It was voiced by the actor Fred Kitchen, and when he died in 1951, the *Times* obituary was headed with the catchphrase. The obituary described him as 'Mr Fred Kitchen, whose cry of triumph as the bailiffs' man, "Meredith, we're in!" echoed for years in every music-hall in the country'. More than 40 years after it was first coined, Kitchen's catchphrase was expected to evoke instant recognition.

Early 2007 saw the publication of a list of top Hollywood phrases of the year. Top of the list were 'High five!' and 'It's sexy time!', both favourite expressions of the supposed Kazakh journalist Borat, actually the comic creation of Sacha Baron Cohen, in the film *Borat*. Another of Baron Cohen's characters, Ali G, has contributed a number of catchphrases to the language. It remains to be seen whether Borat's lines will have the lasting impact of 'Booyakasha!' and 'Respec', but they are certainly proof that the right catchphrase can pack a host of associations that last for years.

The catchphrases of the 2000s

I'm the only gay in the village
– Daffyd in *Little Britain*

Booyakasha!
– *Ali G*

How you doin'?
– Joey in *Friends*

Is that your final answer?
– Host Chris Tarrant in *Who Wants To Be A Millionaire?*

Am I bovvered?
– Lauren in *The Catherine Tate Show*

Deal or No Deal?
– Noel Edmonds, in the game show of the same name

You're fired!
– Alan Sugar in *The Apprentice*

It's sexy time!
– Borat in *Borat: Cultural Learnings of America for Make Benefit Glorious Nation of Kazakhstan*

Ya Burnt!
– *30 Rock*, an American sitcom set in the Rockefeller Plaza

red! **Booyakasha!** Meredith, we're in! **Ya Burnt!** You're fi

Language on the Horizon:
Jottings and Musings

Celebrity coupling

If Pete Doherty and Kate Moss ever decide to get married and 'mesh', they could be known as Mr and Mrs Doss. Tony Blair and George Bush are sometimes said to act like an old married couple, so they could be Mr and Mr Blush.

bbc.co.uk, August 2006.

When Brad Pitt and Angelina Jolie publicly stepped out as a couple, a new epithet for them seemed inevitable: **Brangelina** became the latest in a line of celebrity pairings to attract what some decided to call a 'uni-name'. The first such nickname, at least in very recent memory, was probably **Bennifer**, given to Jennifer Lopez (J-Lo) and Ben Affleck and a gift for tabloid copywriters who monitored the relationship's highs and lows with relish: 'New Lo for Bennifer' was just one of many headlines devoted to the ill-fated couple. One critic described the nickname as 'seemingly encapsulating everything the public felt toward the duo: awe, envy, over-familiarity, even disdain'. Certainly 'Bennifer' took on a life of its own. As Bob Thompson, Professor of Popular Culture at Syracuse University, put it: 'It's as if with those celebrities their celebrity-couple names are the first offspring. Ben and Jennifer didn't leave any children, but they did leave us Bennifer, something they were completely unable to control. It was an unruly child they'd like to have locked up in the attic, but they could never quite catch it.'

When Ben Affleck subsequently married the actress Jennifer Garner, **Ben and Jen** seemed to be one of the few options available, the 'best' having been used already. Tom Cruise and Katie Holmes arguably fared rather better in the name stakes: their nickname, **TomKat**, had a light and affectionate ring to it, continued in the slight adaptation for their new daughter Suri, **TomKitten**.

Nicknames for couples are not, in fact, an entirely new phenomeon. British house names have used such unions for some time. Lucille Ball and Desi Arnaz referred to themselves and their production company as 'DesiLu', while Bill and Hillary Clinton were dubbed 'Billary' by many local radio pundits. These, together with those that will inevitably follow 'Brangelina' and 'TomKat', are like catchphrases picked up from favourite TV characters and slipped into everyday speech, operating as clear signals to our peers that we are 'up' on our celebrity gossip. As a tongue-in-cheek proof of our familiarity with the here-and-now of popular culture, such group identity tags look to be here to stay.

The Queen's English?

In 2004, an article published in the *Journal of Phonetics* announced that the traditional royal speech sounds have undergone subtle changes in the last fifty years, reflecting a shift towards a more democratic style of pronunciation. Jonathan Harrington, Professor of Phonetics at the University of Munich, conducted a thorough acoustic analysis of the Queen's Christmas broadcasts, and concluded that Estuary English, a term coined in the 1980s to describe the spread of London's regional pronunciation features to counties adjoining the river, might well have had an influence on Her Majesty's vowels. 'In 1952 she would have been heard referring to "thet men in the bleck het". Now it would be "that man in the black hat",' the article notes. 'Similarly, she would have spoken of....hame rather than home. In the 1950s she would have been lorst, but by the 1970s lost.'

Such a blurring of boundaries was, for many, a welcome sign of a monarchy more in touch with its people. For others, it was just one more sign of a growing and ugly descent into a dark age of glottal stops. But the Queen is not alone in her receptiveness to the speech habits of modern citizens. Hillary Clinton was criticized during her 2007 campaign tour for adopting a fake 'blackent' to win over the electorate when visiting the Southern States of America. Tony Blair's speeches, too, have frequently prompted comment on their blurred consonants and their use of 'fillers' such as 'you know', 'I mean', and 'honestly'— all much loved by his impersonators.

Such shifts may well be part of an overall trend in our language towards an intimacy which would have been unthinkable only thirty years ago. 'Sometimes I forget I'm Prime Minister,' Blair told the *Sun* shortly after his election to Number 10; 'To me, I'm just Tony Blair.' The voice of authority has clearly changed, and the direction of its pronunciation looks to be towards an even more informal register. Certainly the Queen's grandchildren are leading the way: Zara Phillips and Prince Harry both speak with a pronounced London accent. According to Neil Tweedie in the *Telegraph*, when asked, Her Majesty was 'absolutely neutral' on the subject of her family's growing Estuarization. His December 2006 article concludes: 'Is one bovvered? Does one look bovvered? One thinks not. "A merry Christmas and a happay New Yeah."'

'Sometimes I forget I'm the Prime Minister'

It's all in the vowels

Speaking of sounds, there are definitely some changes afoot in matters of British pronunciation. Chroniclers of dialect have been noting what they term 'GOAT-fronting' by teenagers in Northern England, whereby the traditional northern 'o' sound in 'goat' (and in the traditional song

'When the Boat Comes In') is becoming rather like the sound in 'nurse', resulting in Coke being 'curka curla'.

There is also evidence of the growth across the North of England of a long 'i' sound in words such as 'price', spreading south as far as Sheffield. Long live variation.

The latest from the *OED*

The additions to the *Oxford English Dictionary* are always fascinating. Today, the Dictionary is the subject of a continuous process of revision and updating by a vast team of lexicographers as well as consultants across the English-speaking world, and—as viewers of the TV series *Balderdash and Piffle* will know—new and earlier records of words are being discovered all the time. Since March 2000, the fruits of Oxford's revision work have been published online at quarterly intervals on *OED Online* (www.oed.com).

Some of the new words released in March 2007 are worth noting. **Ta-da**, based on the imitation of a musical sound and the perfect representation of an arrival with a flourish, is evocative and familiar enough today to be used as the title of a recent Scissor Sisters album, while **ixnay** comes from Pig Latin (a coded slang in which children put the beginning of a word at the end), and means 'no way'—it is based on another slang term, *nix*, and has been dated back as far as 1937. Meanwhile it is perhaps appropriate that **wiki**, a web page which can be openly edited by anyone who accesses it (the word is Hawaiian for 'very quick': see pp 100–1), has found a place in the Dictionary. As Graeme Diamond, the *OED*'s New Words Editor, points out, it has been suggested that in some ways the *OED* itself resembles a 'wiki': its long tradition of working on collaborative principles means it has welcomed the contribution of information and quotation evidence from the public for over 150 years.

Finally, the verb **set** has been toppled from its position as the longest entry in the Dictionary. The new leader? The verb to **make**.

Fantastically footballistic

When the Arsenal manager Arsène Wenger pronounced that 'footballistically, it's a surprise' that David Beckham was heading for the US, he cemented in football parlance an adverb he himself coined a few years back and which, delivered with his classic French accent, sounds surprisingly plausible. He is also partial to the adjective 'footballistic' (in France the word *footballistique* is rather more common)—something which, in his view, press criticism of Sven-Goran Eriksson was not. For a sport which is so often criticized for its reliance on cliché—**early bath**, **a game of two halves**, **it's a tale of two goalkeepers**—Wenger's spontaneity stood out as much as the football manager Ian Dowie's **bouncebackability** had a few years before. While the *Oxford English Dictionary* has antedated Dowie's use by 40 years, his popularizing of the word meant that 'bouncebackability' found a place in the new editions of many current English dictionaries in 2006. The Wengerism 'footballistically', on the other hand, looks less likely to step into current language, in spite of its Gallic charms.

'footballistically, it's a surprise'

Hey ho –io

On an even smaller football note, the influence of Chelsea manager José Mourinho (pronounced Mourin-io) may be extending to linguistic corners. Northern Ireland manager Laurie Sanchez recently spoke on Radio Five Live about the prospect of his team playing 'San Marin-io'.

Ating that haitch

In a *Guardian* article in March 2007, David McKie spoke of his dismay at the gradual displacement of 'aitch' as the pronunciation for 'h' by its 'harsher' cousin, 'haitch'. In his book *The Adventure of English*, Melvyn Bragg notes that there was once a primer entitled 'Poor Little H—Its Use and Abuse', which ran to 40 editions.

While h-dropping was long regarded as the mark of the uneducated— witnessed in Eliza Doolittle's gargantuan efforts to haul herself up in life by remembering that 'In **H**ertford, **H**ereford, and **H**ampshire, **h**urricanes **h**ardly ever **h**appen'—it is now a key characteristic of what is still called 'Estuary English'. Whether the changing pronunciation of the letter itself matters is a moot point, but David McKie thinks it does: 'Haitch G Wells sounds to me a more aggressive man, and writer, than Aitch G Wells. An Aitch R Aitch might be expected to proffer a limp regal handshake, where Haitch R Haitch sounds more apt for trouble in nightclubs and service in Iraq.'

The 'N—Haitch—S' *does* sound a bit daunting.

Hinglish, haina?

More people speak English in South Asia than in Britain and North America combined. As a news headline it is not much of a story—the triumph of English as the new rising language was announced back in the late 1900s, and English has been taking on new forms continuously over the 1,500 years or so of its use. But some see these opening years of the 21st century as being a critical moment in the history of our language. In his sequel to his startling 1997 study for the British Council on the future of English, David Graddol in *English Next* predicts that Asia may determine the future of global English, and it may be a very different kind of 'global English' to the one we have been imagining.

The huge increase in the popularity of **Hinglish** is a prime example of the British Council's point. This mix of Hindi and English is now the hippest slang on the streets and college campuses of India. While once considered the resort of the uneducated or of the expatriated—the so-called 'ABCDs' or the American-Born Confused Desi (*desi* denoting a countryman), Hinglish is now the fastest-growing language in the country. So much so, in fact, that multinational corporations have increasingly in this century chosen to use Hinglish in their ads. A McDonald's campaign in 2004 had as its slogan 'What your bahana is?' (What's your excuse?), while Coke also had its own Hinglish strapline 'Life ho to aisi' (Life should be like this). Hinglish has also penetrated the world of Bollywood and films such as *Bend It Like Beckham* and *American Desi*, having become synonymous with all that is hip, chic, and urbane. There are even different Hinglish lexicons. In Bombay, men who have a bald spot fringed by hair are known as **stadiums**, while in Bangalore nepotism or favouritism benefiting one's (male) child is known as **son stroke**.

Inevitably, the tug of Hinglish is being felt in Britain too. In 2006, a new book *The Queen's Hinglish* confirmed the arrival of its vocabulary as well as its colour. Entries included **machi-chips** (fish and chips), **haina** (the new **innit**), **timepass** (a hobby), **prepone** (to bring something forward), **gup-shup** (a chit-chat), and **kissa**. This last word appeared in a much-copied headline from the *Times of India* which ran 'Kissa Kiss Ka' above an article about an offscreen kiss between the singer Mika and the **item girl** (a girl set to become a star having starred in a Bollywood 'item song'—unrelated to the plot but intended to catch on with the public) Rakhi Sawant. The kiss was caught on a mobile phone camera and broadcast over the Internet. *Kissa* actually means 'the story (of something)'.

Creative subtitling

The *Times* has run a report that the plotlines of English-speaking films are becoming garbled because of a lack of linguistic finesse in those countries to which film companies are increasingly outsourcing their subtitling. It suggests that the cost-cutting measure may be backfiring.

The *Times* reported 'lines of dialogue such as, "Jim is a Vietnam vet" have been cruelly mistranslated [sic] as "Jim is a veterinarian from Vietnam"; while, "You've got ivory skin" appears in subtitles as, "You've got skin like an elephant." In a Spanish version of the film *Seabiscuit*, the line '"It was a ball to shoot" became "It was like filming a dance scene".'

'You've got skin like an elephant'

The next day and in the Letters page of the same newspaper, further examples of creative translation were provided. One reader recalled the British version of the French film *Edouard et Caroline*. In it, the character of Caroline answers a call from, she believes, her estranged lover Edouard, and yells: 'Merde merde merde merde merde'—considerately subtitled as 'Blank blank blank blank blank'. Shortly afterwards a friend of Caroline's explains it was he himself who had actually been calling; 'Tu m'as dit "merde",' he tells her. The subtitle put it rather simply: 'You spoke to me in "blank" verse.'

On the blog? Don't be uncouth

The editor-in-chief of *US Vogue* has caused quite a stir by calling for the word **blog** to be banned on account of its vulgarity. She is said to have instructed her staff to find an alternative before the *Vogue* website was launched.

Beyond the inevitable backlash from bloggers themselves came a wider debate about who governs English and particularly about how the language of the Net is determined by 'a small band of technogeeks with a weakness for portmanteau words, bad puns and unwieldy acronyms' (*The Guardian*). 'Blog' itself has been around since 1997 and is simply a contraction of 'web log': it is likely to have arisen out of simple conversation. However inelegant, it has to be one of the strongest surviving coinages of the noughties. Some wags suggested that **blague** might be civilized enough for Anna Wintour, while the *Guardian* mischievously went on to suggest **brant** (= blog + rant) or **twaffle** (= Net + waffle). Whatever the objection, **blog** is a winner.

(Size) zero tolerance

In 2006 the organizers of the Madrid Fashion Week banned any excessively thin models (those with a Body Mass Index of less than 18, considered by medical professionals to mean unhealthily underweight) from the catwalk. The decision catapulted the term **size zero** into popular parlance, and with it the whole debate over the potential effects on the young of the fashion industry's preference for skinny models.

Size zero is a women's clothing size in the US catalogue sizes system. It is the equivalent to a UK size 4. Its rise in currency comes with daily reports on rising obesity levels among the young and the associated health risks. Thanks to the efforts of the celebrity chef Jamie Oliver, **school dinners** also came under the spotlight, with many schools pledging to change their ways for the healthier. Others reported **junk-food mums** passing burgers through the school gates to their children.

In an effort to combat the advance of **globesity** (global obesity), a **fat tax** on junk food has been proposed: in the US such a measure has become known as a **Twinkie tax** (after the finger-shaped sponge cakes with a cream filling).

At the other extreme where 'size zero' resides, skinny models and other celebrities are said to provide **thinspiration** to young women who aspire to be ultra-thin. Such **thinspirational** role models are typically pictured on **pro-ana** and **pro-mia** websites, those which proclaim the 'virtues' of the eating disorders anorexia and bulimia.

The result? Linguistically it is a flood of new words. In the face of such public concern over the pressure on young women to lose weight, it is ironic that the word **anorexia** (which comes from the Greek words *an-* 'without' and *orexis* 'appetite') is experiencing its own form of expansion. The suffix '-rexia' or '-orexia' is being used to generate a host of new terms, including **bleachorexia**: an obsession with whitening the teeth; **tanorexia**: an obsession with maintaining a year-round suntan, especially by using sunbeds; **yogarexia**: an obsession with practising yoga to become or stay slim; **permarexia**: an addiction to faddy slimming diets; **bigorexia**: a disorder whose sufferers believe themselves to be puny even though they are in fact very muscular and who exercise compulsively to increase muscle bulk; and even **brideorexia**: referring to brides-to-be who crash-diet before the wedding so as to look good in the photos.

The casting of doubt-iness

In 2005 the satirical US show *The Colbert Report* introduced the word **truthiness** into American vocabulary. Before long, and thanks in part to its election by the American Dialect Society as its word of 2005, it arrived in Britain as a pithy summary of one of the more dubious aspects of modern life—the 'facts' as we would like them to be rather than what they actually are. Stephen Colbert used his definition of the word, first aired on his show, at a White House Correspondents' dinner, thus implying that the President himself was guilty of what one magazine called 'truth wrapped in truthiness'.

'truth wrapped in truthiness'

The success of the rather clumsy word, which was not entirely new (the *OED* dates it back to the 1800s when it meant a straightforward presentation of the truth) but which was reworked by Colbert, has taken many by surprise. The signs are that it will stick around for a while—particularly as it is being reformulated into other examples of the '-iness' philosophy. **Referenciness** is the new term for the use of authoritative-sounding references which don't quite stand up when followed up. Even **factiness** is beginning to get a look-in. Wordinistas may well predict a future where **wordiness** itself may take on an entirely new meaning.

Try, try, and... tryvertise?

The website *www.trendwatching.com* has suggested this new term for product placement in the real world: where products are introduced into our daily lives so that we can try them out for ourselves rather than believe the advertising claims. The site reports that Sony have included a PlayStation in every room in a top Brighton hotel, while the bath oils and shampoos offered free in even standard hotel rooms are all part of the attempt to win us over. The next step is apparently **try-out stores** dedicated entirely to letting consumers explore new products in recreated domestic settings. If such products are home cinemas or beer taps then we may be creating the hottest form of entertainment in the late noughties: the **insperience**. Linguistic and commercial fads? The jury is out.

'At thee seekin?'

Are dialects lost forever? Many fear so—that we are losing touch with a golden past.

A news story in February 2007 only added to those fears. A heading in the *Scotsman* ran: 'Brothers put in a geed wyord to save an ancient Scottish dialect from extinction.' This introduced the story of two brothers in their eighties, believed to be the last speakers of 'Cromarty fisher dialect'. The rich dialect is thought to be based on the speech that Cromarty people picked up from English soldiers in the 17th and 18th centuries and which spread into the local fishing community. It still uses formal expressions such as 'thee', 'thou', and 'thine', and includes several distinctive sounds, such as the putting in or taking out of an 'h' before many words, so that 'hand' becomes *and* and 'ears' becomes *hears*. 'At thee seekin?' means simply 'What do you want?'

The brothers from Cromarty were making a recording of their speech for the local archives, but it was agreed that the living dialect would pass with their deaths. Many regretted the loss, but others accepted that the story was all part of the natural process of language change— and that as some dialects disappear, other newer ones are recognized. The *Scotsman*'s story was only one half of the picture.

Communication is the key. If a dialect grows out of a particular need which still exists, it will survive. Older dialects which look to be dead can evolve too. In January 2007, the Irish journalist Manchán Magan wrote of his travels around Ireland looking for people who still spoke Gaelic. On the point of giving up, he came across a group of children responding to a radio phone-in programme. They spoke a 'new and modern urban dialect' of Irish. 'They had invented Irish words for X-Box and hip-hop, for jackass and blog. They were fluent in Irish text-speak and had moulded the ancient pronunciations and syntax in accordance with the latest styles of Buffy-speak and Londonstani slang.'

In November 2006, reports ('Poles learning Big Yin's banter' was the *Express*'s headline) of Polish bus-drivers coming to work in the UK included the information that they were being given special help in getting to grips with regional variation. Those going to Glasgow were being shown videos of Billy Connolly. London-bound drivers, meanwhile, got *Only Fools and Horses*.

As the BBC's national *Voices* project showed, there are many local expressions and pronunciations which may well fade along with their speakers. The surprise was that many of these are being given new variations by the young. Individual dialects have a natural life, but the very fact of regional variation is likely to be with us for a long time to come. As they say in the Midlands, 'that's *bostin*'.

Hosing the....what?

When the media frenzy surrounding Prince William's girlfriend Kate Middleton was at its most frantic, a fascinating idiom was popping up everywhere. In paparazzi-parlance, 'hosing the Doris' is the click-click-click of the photographer's lens when a celebrity is in view. The phrase was reported everywhere as a long-established part of photographers' slang. The trouble is, no one knew where the phrase came from, and Google's only reference was to the troubled Ms Middleton. How established could it be? It reveals a fascinating side of language change—a great-sounding phrase becomes a talking point only, on closer inspection, to prove almost completely elusive. Perhaps the new 'waparazzi' citizen journalists will get closer to the truth.

'hosing the Doris'

Be-liscious

When Mars decided on **substantialiscious** as one of the words that best describes their Snickers bar (along with the less convincing 'pea-nutopolis' and 'satisfectellent'), they created one more in a whole line

of coinages with the suffix '-li(s)cious' that
followed on from *Wayne's World*'s **babelicious**
(in that film, Garth and Wayne agree that
Claudia Schiffer is 'magically babelicious' and
tests 'very high on the stroke-ability scale').
Homer Simpson was at it too, declaring the covert
eating of a forbidden waffle **sacrilicious**.

'magically babelicious'

Creating portmanteau words such as these is a natural and fun bit of
wordplay—not as nutty as a Snickers bar.

One foul swoop?

We all know that language moves on. In slang, where words go in and
out of fashion at top speed, changes are pretty obvious: so 'wicked'
came to mean 'good', and 'fit' replaced 'phat' (both meaning
'attractive'). Vocabulary somersaults such as these are at the coalface
of language evolution. But not all change is deliberate—slips of the
tongue can be unwitting but powerful instruments of change. Such
instances of the 'wrong' word replacing the 'right' one over time were
dubbed 'eggcorns' by linguists Geoffrey Pullum and Mark Liberman
in the excellent website *The Language Log*. Liberman had mentioned
a woman who wrote 'eggcorn' rather than 'acorn' as that was how
she heard it in her American regional speech. With that a new term
was born.

Michael Quinion, in his weekly newsletter *World Wide Words* (a joy for
anyone interested in language change), has noted some of the latest
'eggcorns', including a contribution from Jeanette Winterson who was
told by an elderly neighbour that his washing machine had 'given up
the goat'. As Quinion says, we can view them either as a sign of
English going to the dogs, or as part of the natural and intriguing
evolution of the language. Judging by some of the fanciful examples in

the online *Eggcorn Database* and the Oxford English Corpus, creativity is growing like, well, top seed.

'His chickens are coming home to roast.'

'...like a bowl in a china shop'

'They were going at it hammer and thongs.'

'He's putting the cat before the horse.'

'to name a view'

'cut to the cheese'

'I got rid of them in one foul swoop.'

'She succeeded to all intensive purposes.'

Nerdcore

There is gangsta rap, and now there's **geeksta rap**, a new form of rap with lyrics about computer codes and programming language. The track 'Enjoy the Ride', from the Silicon Valley entrepreneur Rajeev Bajaj, gives a flavour:

'Hot electrons can ruin my day
Switch the transistor to go the other way
I make my software self healing
To prevent such a calamity from dealing
A deadly blow to my directory root
If all else fails......YO, REBOOT!'

Some geeksta rap songs look to literary sources such as J.R.R. Tolkien for their material instead of sex or violence. As one Canadian website puts it, however, 'geeksta rappers are no meeker than their inner-city brethren: the f-word appears in nerdcore lyrics almost as frequently as Bilbo Baggins'.

Packing a pithy punch

The columnist Matthew Parris, prompted by a British Airways explanation that Tony and Cherie Blair, who had booked economy-class seats to Florida for their Christmas break, were upgraded to business as any other passenger might have been, commented in the *Times* with a simple 'Yeah, right'. He went on:

> 'Ugly as it is, the American expression "Yeah, right" is a useful recruit to our language's army of colloquialisms. In two words it says what "Pardon me but I find that inherently unlikely, and I think we both know why" says in fifteen.'

Touché (in one).

Bigging it up, still

Linguistic inflation is nothing new—the move away from the 'back to basics' ethos has been hard to escape in the course of the noughties. The overriding trend is towards unnecessary elongation. Bemoaned as far back as 1906, when the Fowler brothers railed against such abuses as 'correctitude' and 'rectitudiness' in *The King's English*, evidence of the current crop is everywhere. Des Browne, Defence Secretary, spoke of **conditionalities** in Iraq, while the expression of **agreeance** on the latest strategy to **operationalize** is common practice in the business world. Budget increases on the prices of cigarettes or fuel are known as **taxations**, **linkage** has routinely replaced 'link', and **methodologies** are the new methods which can **solutionize** rather than solve.

Uprising against such wordiness may be a lost cause. The Fowler brothers thought it banal to talk of **banality**, and that **vulgarity** was vulgar. Neither of these suffers any kind of **conspicuity** today.

Comfort food?

At the same time as food and science forge their partnership and blowtorches, Gastrovacs, and Thermomix become the must-have appliances for any serious cook, the provenance of the food we buy has become crucial. Molecular gastronomy (a term hated by many of the more experimental chefs) may be making the headlines, but it is a far more traditional emphasis which is flavouring the super-market shelves.

For those eschewing battery farms, today's choicest eggs are not just from a particular breed ('Colombian Blacktail' or 'Old Cotswold Legbar'), they are laid by hens that have enjoyed an open-air life among 'small flocks' in the 'pastures' of 'family-run farms'. In one case, the packaging notes that they have been 'bedded on straw' and have had 'ample space to scratch, preen and dust-bathe'. In another instance, we are told that the birds live in 'spacious barns' which have 'windows to allow ample daylight', and that they have 'straw bales to perch on'.

'ample space to scratch'

The lifestyle of other animals also suggests a pastoral idyll. Welsh hill lamb may have been bred on 'pastures that have taken hundreds of years to achieve', while 'deer are free to roam on natural pastures' before being turned into venison sausages. We are also introduced to the farmer, reassured that 'Margaret cares for her chickens'.

Not everyone appreciates such intimacy. In 'You May Kiss the Chef's Napkin Ring', an article in the *New York Times* in January 2007, food critic Frank Bruni protests we can know too much about our food's origin. 'Chef got the eggs from an old lady with cataracts upstate. Chef foraged for the mushrooms in thicket near the Tappan Zee.'

It might be thought that this back-to-the-land movement would have nothing to say to the **foams** and **sous-vide** of molecular gastronomy. However, in October 2006 New York saw a display of cooking by key Spanish chefs. One of them, the Catalan Joan Roca, exhibited a dish whose preparation has been described in the following way: 'The Spanish chef Joan Roca distills essence of dirt from a bucket of mud, then foams the distillate and serves it on an oyster.' This, surely, could literally be described as a down-to-earth approach to food.

7

Boiling Frogs and Burning Platforms:
The Good and Bad of Office English

Most communities have their own linguistic shorthand. And for good reason: the medical profession, where speed is often a life-saving necessity, draws on a staggering array of abbreviations and quick-fire acronyms for medicines and procedures. Firefighters, whose slang includes **flashovers** and **rollovers** (both types of fire), similarly employ a quickly understood code which may be unintelligible to others but vital to themselves. Schoolteachers, chefs, engineers, radio DJs, and long-distance drivers (if a trucker reports that a car has an **alligator** and is **greasy side up**, they might signal a **10-33**—a car with a blown tyre and its wheels in the air is probably an emergency) all rely on a shared language for ease of communication within their group. For many of them, their jargon has the dual purpose of brevity and the tacit acknowledgement of a shared identity. It may also have the highly useful characteristic of being beyond the comprehension of everyone else.

Jargon, then, can be indispensable. It is perhaps puzzling, therefore, that the argot of the business community is the one which is regularly singled out for criticism. Business language, polls regularly tell us, is riddled with empty cliché and with stock phrases which deliver little other than obfuscation (often deliberate) or posturing.

lligator greasy side up blamestorming core competencies

Few would contest that some business jargon, or 'Offlish' as it has been dubbed, can be both infuriating and ridiculous. Many of the words documented in previous *language reports* offer ample demonstration of this. Beyond the familiar **blue-sky** or **joined-up** thinking, **blamestorming**, and **downsizing**, have come and gone an enervating line of words and idioms which are held up as **key indicators** not of success, but of a failed attempt to impress. Yet it is not a few company prospectuses that will boast of **strategic partnerships**, **core competencies**, **business-process outsourcing** (**BPO**), **driving achievement tools**, **improving systems outcomes**, **creating capability**, **managing across the matrix**, and of **blue-prints** or **routemaps** for (a tautological) **future progress**.

The tendency to take perfectly serviceable nouns, verbs, or adjectives and turn them (or **pimp** them, as one critic has described the process, drawing an analogy with souping up a car) into new and rather overblown creations—often a new part of speech altogether—can also give business-speak a bad name. Very recent creations include **conspicuity**, **agreeance**, **operationalize**, **solutioning**, **bandaiding**, **dialoguing**, **rearchitecting**, **leadershipping**, **de-integrating**, and **disincentivizing**. Companies may be **bangalored** (signifying that its call centres have been moved to India as a cost-cutting measure), while its new strategies may be **dialled-** or **baked-in**. Meanwhile, business directors may exhort their employees to have their **feet on fire** on their company's new **burning platforms** (catalysts for urgent change in a drive to remain competitive).

Such over-elaboration—evident also in one company's recently announced decision to improve its **fenestration** (in other words, its windows)—reflects the inflationary attempt to make what is being said sound more impressive. The effect is usually the opposite, particularly when statements tip over into cliché. Be it **empower-ment**, the **visionary process**, or **passion statements**, the evidence of 'talking up' is everywhere. Nor is it always harmless—business jargon designed to make a harsh reality more palatable, as in talk of **recalibrating** personnel (i.e. firing them), attracts particular censure. As in politics, euphemism is indispensable: the airline easyJet recently told the *Today* programme, following disappointing results, that they had experienced not a drop in revenue but a **softening of yield**.

All of which suggests that the criticism for which the business world is often singled out is, in fact, fair. What is overlooked, however, is the other face of Offlish: a cheerful inventiveness that resolutely defies reliance on over-worn phrases. Idioms which have made an entrance over the course of the last five years include **opening/lifting the kimono** (revealing hitherto privileged information), **leg-lifting** (arguably much more entertaining than the act it describes, namely selling one part of a combination share while keeping the remaining part), **kitchen-sinking** (announcing all of a company's bad financial results at one time: a term alluding back to the idiom 'everything but the kitchen sink'), **square-headed girl-friend** (a computer), **prairie-dogging** (spying over a colleague's cubicle partition wall, looking as a prairie dog guarding its colony might do), as well as the by now infamous **boiling frog syndrome** (applied to a company which fails to recognize gradual market change, just as a slowly-boiled frog may not detect a slow tempera-ture increase) and **elephant in the room/moose on the table** (a problem which everyone at a meeting is aware of, but which no one dare speak of). Few could contest their humour and splash of colour.

Indeed humour such as this is present in much of the business lexicon, even if it is the more informal version. More recently noted are tongue-in-cheek items such as **word-of-mouse** (for interest generated by the volume of online visitors to a company's website), **lipstick on a pig** (an attempt to put a favourable spin on a negative situation), a **pig in a python** (a surge in a statistic measured over time), **yogurt cities** (targeted by companies who wish to appeal to their 'culture'), **fluff it and fly it** (to make cosmetic changes to something before selling it), and **royal jelly** (flashy projects fed to someone whom the boss is grooming for promotion). The latter, clearly the coinage of disgruntled co-workers, sits alongside other employee-inspired terms such as **carpool tunnel syndrome** (the boredom of sharing a car with a fellow worker), **competimates** (companies forced into an uneasy alliance in a joint venture), and **deceptionist** (used to describe a receptionist or secretary whose job it is to delay or block potential visitors on behalf of their boss). Conversely, the verb **sunset**, as in 'let's sunset that idea' (i.e lay it to rest), and the new version of the **brainstorm** (now considered to be politically incorrect due to the term also being used medically for a neurological affliction), the **thought shower**, both sound very much like inventions from the top.

As in the firefighting and medical professions, there exists in business a shorthand designed for brevity for those in the know. Straightforward abbreviations and acronyms are among the areas of business-speak that move most quickly, as they are often the expression of new technologies which will themselves be quickly superseded. Within the mobile phone industry, **RFID** (radio frequency identification), **NFC** (near-field communication), **GSM** (the global system for mobile communications), and **VAD** (voice activity detection) are just four of thousands of contractions designed to aid quick communication. Far from being overelaborate jargon, they are indispensable: without them, effective dialogue within the industry and in particular across international boundaries would be almost impossible.

Does the language of commerce deserve its bad name? The answer is partly. Much of management-speak seems designed, to borrow George Orwell's words on political discourse, to 'conceal or prevent thought' rather than express it. So much so that the new boardroom game of the 21st century is **buzzword** (or, less politely and rather more clandestinely, **bullshit**) **bingo**, in which attendees each have a matrix of buzzwords from which they cross off any word spoken in a meeting. The winner is the person who first crosses off a full line. And yet there is much business vocabulary that does the job for which it is intended. Some words even entertain at the same time. For a language so often accused of an over-reliance on the hackneyed, Offlish continues to enjoy one of the highest rates of turnover in current language. Perhaps if the linguistic aim is the same as the commercial one, namely to be alert to the new and to be creative, all will be far from lost.

zword **Offlish** buzzword bingo **BlackBerry** Offlish manag

8

Online English: The New Normal

We're 14 hours into no BlackBerry, so you can imagine how things are. We've already started a 12-step group.

White House spokesman Tony Fratto in April 2007, after the BlackBerry service went down across North America causing national dismay.

I had my own blog for a while, but I decided to go back to just pointless, incessant barking.

A *New Yorker* cartoon by Gregory depicting two dogs in conversation, September 2005.

At the time of the first *language report* in 2002, it was already very clear that the impact on language of the online explosion was going to be huge. The Internet and its dominions were fast generating both new vocabulary and new ways of using it. Five years on, and from the perspective of this year's report, the vista is dramatically different. Few would have predicted that the very success of the Internet has meant that its influence in neologizing has decreased. For in the increasingly online first years of the 21st century, *online language* is becoming the norm rather than an area of difference.

The term **online** originally referred to those special and expensive times when a computer was connected to a network via, literally, a telephone line. Working 'offline' was the norm: it gave the benefits of word processing and so on, without a sense of being deprived of key information. Today's norm is very different, thanks to the exponential increase of authoritative information available on the Web. If an Internet connection fails today, the offer of working 'offline' is still there, but the sense of deprivation is deep. If we let the term 'online' include BlackBerries and mobile phones, then we spend very little time out of reach of a network.

Paradoxically, this has probably limited the amount of new vocabulary generated online: if everyone is online, online is nowhere special. In this sense the online world now is recognizably different from that of the first *language reports*, when interacting online was more of a novelty.

This is not to deny that there are some online areas which immediately suggest themselves as potentially rich sources of new vocabulary. **Second Life** is an online three-dimensional virtual reality, in which millions of users communicate with each other, and create (virtual) objects, possibly even selling them to other 'residents' using the in-world currency. The world is a sealed one, the language of which rarely steps over into the real world. *Second Life* 'residents' refer to their in-game invented identities as **avatars**, and they may worry about various types of **lag** caused by slow connections or server loads. However, both these terms comfortably predate *Second Life*, and for such a distinct community there is rather little new vocabulary. The new terms which have emerged are largely technical, including **rez** (meaning 'to create or render an object') and **prim** (a contraction of the 'primitive' objects from which the avatars' appearances are built up).

line Second Life avatars lag rez prim pwn fragging on

Role-playing games (**RPG**s), meanwhile, also have some specialized vocabulary exclusive to their online world. This includes the 'leetspeak' **pwn**, referring to domination of one player by another (in which case they get **pwned**), and **frag**, referring to an in-game kill and borrowed from US military slang in which it denotes throwing a fragmentation grenade at an unpopular senior officer. **Leetspeak** itself is a distinct online dialect, a written form of coded slang which uses specific letters or numbers to replace proper letters.

'Leetspeak', and other codes like it, are among the few remaining examples of language which is truly and exclusively 'online'. Most of the vocabulary in the conversations in role-playing games, as in *Second Life*, *MySpace*, and other online forums, is not—or at least is no longer—a special online language: it draws instead on the by now well-known contractions and slang of SMS (text-) speak.

If the term 'online language' is becoming something of a misnomer, the influence of the Internet and its diverse communities on English have been dramatic, and the extent to which they have shaped our language incontrovertible. The language of the virtual world no longer appears in exclusively online locations. It has penetrated the real world in terms both of usage and of individual items of vocabulary.

The word **blog** is one of the most prominent neologisms to be created this century. While it refers to an online venture—an online diary or 'web log' of personal experiences and opinions—blogging is still very much about the real, 'offline', world which bloggers inhabit. Such is the success of the phenomenon (which has surely been influenced by the equal popularity of the word) that few of us today would be unaware of its meaning. Coined in the closing years of the 20th century, *blog* was still something of a novelty at the time of the first *language report*. Today, the growing number of linguistic spin-offs are ample demonstration that 'blog' is a survivor. From the original term have sprung **moblog** and **phlog** (a mobile phone plog, and a photographic blog), **vlog** (video blogging), **splog** (a spam-like technique for exploiting inter-blog references), **plog** (a political blog), and **flog** (which can be glossed in multiple ways, including a 'fake blog').

A **podcast** is another highly successful word which, although again an activity made possible by online technology, has made significant inroads into our everyday lexicon. From a technical point of view, a podcast is almost indistinguishable from a blog: both have a **feed**—a short file encapsulating recent changes to the blog, processed and displayed by an **aggregator**—but while the blog's content is text, that of the podcast is audio. The word is patterned after 'broadcast', but with 'pod' deriving from Apple's iPod MP3 player. Apple has tried, largely successfully, to prevent 'pod' and 'podcast' becoming generic terms in the same way as 'hoover' and 'kleenex', but the high turnover of spin-offs presents considerable linguistic opposition. The term **vodcast** has been used to refer to podcasts with video components (and seems to be a synonym for 'vlog' above), a **godcast** is a religious broadcast for downloading, **mobpodcast** is a portmanteau of 'moblog' and 'podcast', and **blogcast** of 'blog' and 'podcast'. As with the more exotic variants of 'blog' above, a lot of these terms seem too deliberately created, and too clumsy to say, to have much of a future. However, the very fact of their creation is testimony to 'podcasting' being a winning choice as a word for this new technology.

Another term which has gone from a curiosity five years ago to a commonplace today is **wiki**. The first 'WikiWikiWeb' was created in

1995 by the US computer programmer Ward Cunningham, who named it using the Hawaiian word *wiki-wiki*, meaning 'very quick'. A wiki is a website which lets users edit its pages. Although has been used in many contexts over the years, it is best known now as the technology behind **Wikipedia** and **Wiktionary**, the online encyclopedia and dictionary. Once more, spin-offs suggest staying power as well as success. **Wikiality** is a fairly new term for reality as defined by a consensus in a collaborative endeavour such as a wiki or Wikipedia. **Wikification** is the process of inviting visitors to a website to openly edit its content.

The thing that links podcasts and wikis is that they both represent **user-generated content** (**UGC**). Though this sounds highly jargonistic, it is the central notion in what has become known, in a much disputed phrase, as **web 2.0**. Rather than having **content** generated by or on behalf of a publisher (as is the case with this book, for example), web-2.0 enterprises—the **read-write web**—aim to have the content which attracts users to their site generated by those users themselves. Wikipedia is again the most obvious noncommercial example of this, while *Second Life*, *MySpace*, *Flickr*, and *del.icio.us* are free to use but owned by commercial organizations. Both of the latter two sites crucially encourage users' **tagging** (associating brief electronic labels with websites or photos in the expectation that they will help you or others find them in future), facilitate **social bookmarking** (the same notion, but emphasizing its collaborative aspects) and thus **folksonomies** (the observation that the set of **tags** that are generated this way constitute an informal popular taxonomy).

Another web 2.0 notion is the **mashup**, a term appropriated from the offline world. Although the word originally referred to a piece of music created by sampling other pieces, in the web world it refers

viki web 2.0 **tagging** social bookmarking **mashup** read-w to a web application which is created by pulling together other independent applications, in the way that *placeopedia.com*, for example, pulls together Wikipedia information with Google Maps imaging.

'Tagging', 'content', and 'bookmarking' are all examples of the way in which the Internet borrows words from 'outside' and retools their traditional meaning for a new environment. Their new specialized connotations are key to understanding the way that the web has changed in the last few years.

The 'noughties' have seen huge increases in both global and domestic **bandwidth**: the word **broadband** is commonplace now, although it would have been very esoteric even five years ago. The vast increase in available bandwidth has meant a proportionate rise in the content available to us. Not all of which is desirable for commercial organizations. **Filesharing** networks, usually comprising music and video files, have flourished, and a large fraction of them are transported without the copyright owner's permission. It is for this reason that words and phrases like **copyright**, **intellectual property** (IP), **digital rights management** (DRM), and **licence** have become key terms in the discussion of the future of the Internet. Like 'bookmarking' and 'tagging', they are words that are moving towards greater frequency of usage in the online, rather than the offline, world.

Life online has its share of dangers: new opportunities for all include new opportunities for mischief. One online menace that is known to all computer users is **spam**, named, for its ubiquity, after the Monty Python 'Spam' song. Spam is a serious problem, not only because of its volume (it is estimated that 80% of all email messages around the world are spam), but because of the frauds contained in the spams, and the illegal activities of the spammers. A large proportion of spams are **phishing** frauds, whereby a fraudster attempts to trick the recipient of the spam into entering their bank or credit-card details into a lookalike website that the spammer has set up. The term 'phishing' is a mutation of 'fishing', and has produced the derivatives **vishing** and **smishing/smsishing**, denoting the same type of fraud using Voice Over IP and SMS messages respectively. Spams are usually sent in bulk from **botnets**: large networks of **zombie** machines which the spammers have gained control over, by using a **trojan** or a **virus**. Not unexpectedly, the lexicon of illegal activity has expanded rapidly in this opening decade of the 21st century.

The Internet has, just as predicted, revolutionized our lives and our vocabulary. Previous *language reports* have emphasized the variety of language within it: far from offering one homogenous way of communicating from a single lexicon, the online world is full of individual communities, each of which created their own 'dialect'. The surprise is that the previously clear boundaries between the language of the online and offline worlds are becoming blurred. So much so, in fact, that by the end of the first decade of this new century the term 'online language' may well be an anachronism.

Whatever happens, the medium of the Internet and all it offers will continue to be one of the greatest—perhaps *the* greatest—orchestrators of language change, not least because of the dazzling speed with which it is evolving.

mbie **botnets** trojan **bandwidth** filesharing **spam** phishi

The top online words this century

alloneword: this isn't really a new word, but rather a new locution often required to pass on websites and email addresses whose names are composed of multiple words: someone might say 'Just look at WWW dot askoxford-alloneword dot com'.

blog: surely one of the main new online words of the century, indicating just how many people want to write something which, for one reason or another, good and bad, would never get published in the 'old media'. Many—perhaps most—blogs don't talk about a specificallly online world, and are an online phenomenon only in the tangential sense that it is the online world that lets these offline thoughts make it into public view.

mashup: this is the read-write web's keyword, representing all the ways in which disparate online resources can be combined in unexpected ways.

read-write web: whether it's called the 'read-write web' or 'web 2.0', the (rediscovered) notion that everyone should be able to write to the web, as well as read it, will probably do more to upset old media than anything else the web has produced so far.

wiki and **Wikipedia:** possibly the most successful outcomes of the above.

podcasting: another neologism which established itself with amazing speed at the same time as inviting numerous spin-offs.

iki **alloneword** mashup **read-write web** podcasting Wikip

words in the spotlight

daemon

News reports in April 2007 carried the story that the film studio New Line Cinema had added an interactive feature to the website for their forthcoming film *The Golden Compass*, based on the first book in Philip Pullman's *His Dark Materials* trilogy. The feature was called 'Meet your Daemon'. In Pullman's stories, his heroine Lyra and everyone from her world has an accompanying spirit in the shape of an animal—their *daemon*. The 'daemon' gives form to what in traditional religious language might be called the 'soul'.

By choosing the word Philip Pullman has given a particular meaning and association to a term which otherwise was likely to be known only in much more limited use. 'Daemon' is an archaic spelling of *demon* (reflecting its Greek origin), which fell out of general use by the end of the 19th century. It was retained in ancient Greek belief as a term for a supernatural being, and it was used as a term for an inner spirit. The writer Rudyard Kipling used it as a name for his personal literary inspiration: in his autobiography, *Something of Myself* (1936), he wrote: 'My Daemon was with me in the *Jungle Books*, *Kim*, and both *Puck* books, and good care I took to walk delicately, lest he should withdraw.'

The associations of 'daemon' are literary and classical; as such they fit very well with the complex and fascinating universe of Philip Pullman. Today, 'daemon' even has an extended use in computing, designating a background process that handles requests for services such as file transfers and is dormant when required. But it is surely thanks to the enormous success of Pullman's creations that the word has been brought back firmly into the limelight.

9

The Old, the New, the Borrowed, and the Blue

Slang is ... a pile of fossilised jokes and puns and ironies, tinselly gems dulled eventually by overmuch handling, but gleaming still when held up to the light.

Anthony Burgess, British novelist and essayist, *A Mouthful of Air*, 1992.

Slang, by those who use it, is held to be the linguistic ultimate. Whether it's **hip**, **cool**, **bling**, **awesome**, **tight**, **rad**, **wicked**, **sick**, **gnarly**, **dope**, **fresh**, or **pimp**, the modern slang lexicon has a vast store of adjectives to describe it. As probably the fastest-moving area in our language, slang proclaims itself to be cutting-edge, young, street, *now*. But is this instinctive view of our informal language, what the American author Louis Untermeyer called 'the shorthand of the people', really as new as it seems?

For all its self-definition as the very latest linguistic event, slang in fact gets no special pleading. Paradoxical as it seems, the very subset of the English language which is seen as the ultimate in modernity is often not so much striding bravely forward, but running (albeit quickly) on the same spot. A major reason for this is that the subjects for slang are both constant and surprisingly few. When we look at the near-hundred-thousand slang words and phrases that have accumulated over the past five centuries and which we are able to trace back, we find a tight group of themes. Uppermost among these are sex, drugs, alcohol, cruelty, and vulgarity. As the American lexicographer and slang collector J E Lighter put it: 'A truly unexpurgated collection of slang reminds us that the world of discourse, like the world of sense, is savage as well as sublime.' Slang is a narrow waterfront, indeed, but it is one which is seriously deep.

Much of slang is about wordplay. One of the simplest forms this takes is turning words head-over-heels and subverting their meaning entirely. One obvious example is the formula of **bad** meaning 'good'. In the sixties the Shangri-Las were singing 'Hmm, he's good-bad but he's not evil...', while more recently celebrity interviews have been frequently punctuated with **wicked**, **nasty**, **sick**, **pimp**, **treach**, **scandalous**, or **vicious**—all of which have turned up in the last decade or so and in every case have turned a word that in standard use is negative into one of approbation.

The role of such subversion, and this is true of all slang, is to keep others guessing. Slang is a code which keeps those in the know in, and those who are not, out. As soon as the code is cracked and outsiders (often parents) scale the wall, then a new word is needed. In fact, the primary force behind slang is the need for a code, whether as an essential means of subterfuge in the criminal under-world (where Cockney rhyming slang began for just that reason) or as a marker of identity. The newness of slang is more a by-product of that need: the initial intent is to establish a group language and, crucially, to keep outsiders out. It is a game which has been played for centuries. **Rum**, a word that first appeared around 1621, first meant 'good, fine, excellent'. A *rum duke* was an unusually handsome man. The word began in Romany use and was most probably from the name of Rome (and indeed could be spelled 'rome' until the 18th century), which as a city meant glory and grandeur; hence as a slang term it came to mean excellent, first-rate. By the late 18th century, however, *rum* had been turned on its head. The reputation of Romanies as criminals may have been the factor in causing *rum* to change into its very opposite. What had been good was bad, or at least eccentric and strange.

Rum today is fairly moribund, whether meaning good or bad, but its linguistic pattern persists. Even the use of *bad* to mean good is itself something of a veteran, with early examples found around 1900. Australian convicts, as the authorities complained, had been reversing *good/bad* a whole century earlier: calling a criminal a *good* man and an overseer *bad*.

If you are *bad*, you are also most likely to be **cool**. *Cool* is another still hotly popular adjective that seems impervious to time. Setting aside its weather implications (that sense of *cool* is a millennium old), the slang use has been around for a good century. 'Cool' was already being used as a synonym for nonchalance and sangfroid in 1816. The modern affirmative use seems to originate with the 1890s Etonian slang *a cool fish*, one who was cocky and self-possessed. It was popularized by the *cool* jazz movement of the 1940s, and epitomized in Charlie Parker's record 'Cool Blues' of 1947, thus cementing the word in modern vocabulary. Having gone quiet for a few decades it has returned with force into today's teen (and older) slang lexicon.

Unlike *bad* and its peers, **homie** (or **homes** or **homey**) is, to pun on another item of modern slang, **all good**. Again, however, it isn't quite as newly minted as one might imagine. Its first use appears in records from early 20th-century Australia, when it referred to a British immigrant, especially one newly arrived or still nostalgic for

ie wicked **bad** pimp **treach** rum **vicious** cool homie ba the 'home country'. Today's use stems from black America, and that too began as a reference to someone missing 'down home'; it was only later, around the 1940s, that it came to be a slang synonym for 'friend'. *Homey* springs from *homeboy*, a term which is a good deal older yet. From its original meaning of a 'stay-at-home', it took on the sense of a person from one's own home town or neighbourhood (both meanings date from the late 19th century). By the 1960s it had picked up its modern meanings: someone who has come to the city from the same rural or provincial area as oneself, a fellow black person, or a young black or Hispanic member of a street gang. 'Homey' remained very much within the rich slang lexicon of the black community, until hip-hop pushed so much of its vocabulary into the general slang arena.

The prominence of the term **booty** has been unmistakable in the 21st century. The popular and thriving online slang collection that is the *Urban Dictionary* offers some 200 combinations of the word, the best-known of which are probably **bootylicious** (gorgeous and sexy), **booty call** (a telephone call made for the sole purpose of inviting sex), and **booty bandit** (a prison homosexual). Although 'booty' sounds like buttocks, or its slang equivalent *butt*, it in fact originated in the standard English term *body* and yet again predates today's youthful use. It referred initially (in around 1908) to female sexuality. Uses meaning the buttocks, and by the 1960s the body, irrespective of gender, were added later.

Butter or **butters** is another term very much associated with the slang of the moment but which has some mileage, even if, by originating in the 1970s, its heritage is not as old as many. On the one hand it can mean 'good': its roots lie in 'smooth as butter'. Far more often, in today's teenspeak, it has the more unpleasant sense of a girl whose face doesn't match the charms of her figure. In this case it may come from a linguistic joke: 'She's got a nice body, but her *face*….', but as the adjective is applied to both genders a more likely origin is 'butt-ugly'.

Pants, once an all-purpose put-down, is not what it was—Bridget Jones, the great popularizer of the term, has presumably moved on to other epithets—but it can still be heard very often, and particularly in the conversational slang of those in their twenties and thirties. Once again it suggests that slang, while it moves quickly, so often looks back on itself to find the new word of the day. In this case the jury is out as to whether the modern sense of 'pants' is a neologism or a resurrection of an older term. Admittedly there is a gap between what seems to be the earliest use of the adjective and its contemporary use: the *Atchison* (Kansas) *Daily Globe* of 19 February 1887 includes the line: 'When the Last Day comes he will find that his name is Pants.' There are plenty more such examples, in which 'pants' is always coupled with 'name': here the meaning may be restricted to the US sense of 'trousers', but in the UK there is no doubt of the connection between underpants and the modern slang sense. A hundred years on from the Kansas *Globe*, 'pants' became one of the top disapproving adjectives of choice among the young. In 2001, the slogan for the BBC's Comic Relief charity telethon ran 'Say Pants to Poverty', thus confirming the hipness of the word which had been re-popularized by Radio 1 DJs since the mid 1990s, and particularly by Simon Mayo, whose own catch-phrase was 'It's a pile of pants!' If the debate still runs over whether Mayo coined this new sense of 'pants' to mean a load of rubbish—others credit another Radio 1 DJ Zoe Ball—he certainly put it back in the slang dictionary. Thanks to its re-airing, the phrase 'it's a pile of pants' was most definitely cool.

Props comes from *proper*, or more fully, *proper respect*. The first examples actually use 'propers', thus one from 1972: 'If you're as cool as I think you is, just give Fatima her propers.' 'Props' doesn't take over until the 1990s, but thereon in it rules the roost. It is a prominent example of the enormous influence of Black American English on 20th- and 21st-century slang. Today's coinages, even from the most inaccessible streets of New York or Los Angeles, are in the mouths of British teenagers within weeks. Rap culture and hip-hop music in particular have accelerated the take-up of American slang in the rest of the English-speaking world.

The list of slang terms which have made it big this century is extensive, and in many cases, the past is still elbowing up against the present. But this is not to diminish the power of slang, whether modern or vintage. The reality is that for all the easy dismissals of slang's apparent ephemerality, the truth is quite otherwise. Not everything can rival *booze*, which has been in slang (and then general) dictionaries since 1566, but the slang lexicon does offer wide stability. Once enough time has passed, there is little hindrance to recycling older words. The original gang of users, and the term's wider recognition, will be long gone. Indeed, given that perhaps three quarters of all the slang that has ever been noted down is still in use, the vitality of this parallel language, and its linguistic exuberance, cannot be in doubt. The novelist and dramatist John Galsworthy wrote in 1927 that 'slang is, at least, vigorous and apt. Probably most of our vital words were once slang'. In fact, many of our vital words still are.

booze **phat** minging **crib** rad **random** fly **the shiznit** inni

The slang terms of the century

cool

phat (attractive)

butters (ugly)

minging (ugly; undesirable)

props (respect)

homie (friend)

crib (home; house)

rad (short for 'radical': naturally cool or stylish)

random (crazy, offbeat, strange)

dope (hip, cool)

fresh (trendy; very good)

lush (attractive)

groovy (very good; cool)

fly (excellent)

wicked (excellent)

gnarly (extreme, excellent, or amazing)

sick (cool, excellent)

tight (stylish, cool)

the shiznit (the business)

innit (isn't it?/am I?/aren't they?/are you? etc.)

nang (cool)

buff (attractive; fit)

minging crib rad random fly the shiznit innit buff min

words in the spotlight

hallows

One of the most fascinating things about language is that you can never safely predict which words may catch the public attention. Up to 2006, **hallows** might have seemed an unlikely candidate. Etymologically, it comes from the same root as 'holy'. *Hallow* as a verb, meaning 'to honour as holy', or 'to consecrate', is most likely to be encountered in formal or literary contexts. The traditional form of the Lord's Prayer includes the words 'hallowed be thy name'. Less seriously, the grass surface of a well-known sporting venue might be referred to as 'hallowed turf', as in reports of the opening of the revamped Wembley Stadium in the spring of 2007.

In Anglo-Saxon England, *hallow* as a noun meant 'a saint' or 'a holy person'. All Saints' Eve was sometimes called 'All Hallows' Eve'—which gives us the familiar name of *Halloween*.

In 2007, J K Rowling's final volume in the Harry Potter series added another chapter to the history of *hallows*. In Potter's world, the Deathly Hallows are three mythical, magical objects which bestow great power, and which include the legendary cloak of invisibility.

10

Sold in a Sentence:
The Art of the Headline

Critic of Queen punched in face; 'Take that!' cries her defender; Lord Altrincham is waylaid by ex-seaman on street after appearing on TV

New York Times, 7 August 1957, after Lord Altrincham criticized the Queen, thereby inviting protest from the Archbishop of Canterbury and heads of State as well as a member of the League of Empire Loyalists.

The British, or at least the British elite, have always read about their wars in the *Times*. And if anything was worth emblazoning across the front page of a national newspaper, a battle for the immediate military security of the country would probably be it. In the lead-up to the battle of Waterloo and after, the *Times* carried bulletins—sometimes as many as six a day—from their correspondent in Brussels, Baron de Capellen. The reports filtered through around five days after the events had taken place and were announced only by the simplest headlines at the top of single columns, such as 'News from Army'. The one printed on 23 June 1815 which described the 'complete' victory at Waterloo on the 18th was headed **Brussels Papers**. Not a great deal had changed, apart from the speed with which reportage travelled, when the *Times* reported the end of the First World War on 12 November 1918. Coverage of that event unsurprisingly dominated the paper, but the biggest actual headline was **Harrods Blouse Week**. By 4 September 1939, however, some elements of a modern headline were apparent, when the paper announced Britain's declaration of war on Germany with a distinctly more emotive headline which crossed two columns: **Britain's Fight to Save the World**.

None of these headlines was on the front page, which throughout this period was reserved by the *Times* for announcements of births, marriages, and so on. So it was significant when over the course of the Second World War important news did start to penetrate the front page in headline form, even though the reports themselves still had to give place to the traditional announcements. On 2 May 1945, the front page included a prominent, fully capitalized addition to the masthead: **Hitler Dead**. Similarly six days later the paper announced: **End of War in Europe**. Finally, if we go forward to 1982 and Britain's most recent national conflict, we find on 15 June, across the front page and in bold type, a real headline: **Ceasefire Agreed in the Falklands**. Of course, the *Times* was by virtue of its very status a conservative publication, and just over a month before the end of the Falklands War, on 4 May 1982, the British tabloid *The Sun* had run perhaps the archetype of the modern headline on its report of the sinking of the Argentinian cruiser General Belgrano by a British submarine: **Gotcha**. How did headline writing get from 'Brussels Papers' to 'Gotcha'?

To understand what happened we need to turn to the United States. On 4 July 1863, the *New York Times* reported on the Battle of Gettysburg, which had raged in Pennsylvania for the previous three days. It ran the headline **The Great Battles** across the first column of the front page. In terms of the development of the banner headline, it was already at the stage which the *Times* took a further 70 years to

reach. American headlines became not simply factual, but dramatically so. On the day after VJ Day (15 August 1945, celebrating the victory in Japan that ended World War II) the New York *Post-Standard* ran a massive banner across its front page, shouting **Victory!** in a way recognizably akin to the *Sun*'s scream of **Gotcha**. Indeed, the term 'banner headline' was coined in the States at the beginning of the 20th century, and the word *headlinese*, describing the formulaic and somewhat unnatural language of headline writing, appeared there after the First World War.

Much of the move was down to business imperatives. In the competitive commercial environment of the US newspaper industry, editors and proprietors wanted their headlines to shout as loudly as possible. In Britain, the more commercially-minded tabloids followed American style much more promptly than the 'qualities'; the *Daily Mirror* reported on the assassination of Bobby Kennedy under the words **God! Not Again!**

There is a more subtle connection, however, between the development of modern headlines in the States and the turnover of the newspaper publishers. The headline exploited the much greater informality (indeed creativity) in the distinctively American use of English. For example, the most successful Americanism of all, *OK*, was first brought to prominence in the reporting of the 1840 American Presidential election. Headlines such as **We Rise to Conquer—Coeymans O.K.** (a report in Albany's *Rough-hewer* of a local victory for the paper's preferred candidate, Martin Van Buren) would have been unthinkable in Britain in terms of both vocabulary and style, even in a local newspaper. Throughout the second half of the 19th century, the vivid nicknames of American political slang were firmly within the scope of headline writers, especially in New York: **A Plug-Ugly Contemporary**, said the *New York Daily Times* on 10 October 1857 at the top of a piece on the famous street gang whose name became a byword for political persuasion; **Mugwump Bradley wins**, announced the New York *Sun* of a 1904 election.

This latter example illustrates a key linguistic feature in the headline's development. The so-called attributive use of nouns, where one noun is placed in front of another, was taken up for its brevity and its punchiness. This was in effect a reinvention of a technique which derives from English's very nature as a Germanic language, and which has been part of English's poetic heritage since *Beowulf*. Over the course of the 20th century, such formations increasingly found their way into British headlines. Even the *Times* referred to the crew of Apollo 11 as **Moon men** in 1969. As well as the use of monosyllabic words wherever possible, this last example also illustrates another characteristic of modern headlines which has its roots deep in the poetic heritage of the English language—the prominence of alliteration. When a similar combination occurs the result is almost always attention-catching. On 2 November 1906, the *Los Angeles Times* ran a story on a cyclist being knocked over by a car (something novel and newsworthy in those days) under a headline which employed a combination of attributive noun use, alliteration, and even a nod towards the rhyming headlines which have developed much more recently. The result was a headline that was arresting, intriguing, and astonishingly modern: **Chug Chugger Rib Smasher**.

The importance of puns and jokes in modern headlines is well known. Frequently, these puns stretch both credulity and the English language to near breaking point; but the best are both very clever and economically effective in that they deliver to the reader the humour and entertainment which often underpins their choice to buy that paper rather than another—the sense that life is indeed always better in the *Sun*. Of the best, the reporting of the Queen's 'annus horribilis' as **One's Bum Year** vies with the description in February 2000 of Celtic's surprise Scottish FA Cup football defeat to Inverness Caledonian Thistle as **Super Caley go Ballistic, Celtic are Atrocious** (a 14-syllable pun on the song from the *Mary Poppins* musical). A very similar headline, and arguably one of the best of 2007, is **Who do You Think You are Kidding, Mr Ahmajinebad?**, responding to the parading of the British naval captives by the Iranian government. The reference in this case is to the song 'Who do you think you are kidding Mr Hitler?', which gives the headline an additional double pungency. It makes a serious point by linking the Iranian government with Nazi Germany, but also relates itself to a particular comic strand of British popular culture, the song being the theme tune to the classic BBC sitcom *Dad's Army*. The use of cultural reference for both serious and comic effect has also begun to find a place in the British broadsheets; for example, in February 2007, the *Times* headlined a report on an outbreak of bird flu at a Bernard Matthews turkey farm with **It's not so Bootiful**, playing on the well-known strapline of the company's marketing strategy. In November 2006, the news that the former Russian spy Alexander Litvinenko had probably been poisoned with radioactive polonium-210 at a London restaurant was headlined by the *Sun* as **From Russia with Lunch**.

This kind of wordplay and use of cultural reference is its own form of poetry, and the sense of poetry does not stop there. If a pun is unmakable, it is always worth throwing in a rhyme, especially if that rhyme involves either popular slang or words which don't actually exist. In 2004, the *Daily Star* responded to a judicial report's criticism of the Home Secretary's plans for extending the use of electronic tagging with **Judge Slags Tag-a-lag**. A recent *Sun* headline referring to the girlfriend of footballer Wayne Rooney was

Schoolgirl Chav to Gladrag Wag. These rhymes are another important aspect of stylization in modern headline writing.

From 'Brussels Papers' to 'Gotcha' seems like a long journey. In fact, the subject matter and the attempt to sell a story are not so different. Perhaps the crucial distinction is that today, we expect our headline writers to entertain as well as to inform. The linguistic devices they use to do so have a surprisingly long heritage—the image of the headline writer as poet may not be so far-fetched after all.

A selection of headlines from 2007

Big Bigot

Daily Mirror, 16 January, passing judgement on Jade Goody who was accused of racist bullying on the reality TV show *Celebrity Big Brother*.

Posh and Bucks

The Sun, 21 January, on footballer David Beckham's decision to sign with the Los Angeles Galaxy team for a reported $50 million a year.

The State of The President: Beleaguered

The Washington Post, 24 January, after President Bush's State of the Union address in which he tried 'to revive his presidency against what may be the greatest odds any chief executive has faced in a generation'.

He's Just Not Into Ewe

The New York Times, 25 January, reporting on research into what makes some sheep gay.

Freddie—You Stupid Bugger!

Daily Mirror, 21 March, after England's cricket vice-captain Freddie Flintoff ended a boisterous evening during the World Cup by falling out of a pedalo (an act which became known as 'fredalo'). He was subsequently sacked as vice-captain and banned from the next match.

What the Gord Giveth, the Gord Taketh Away

Daily Mail, 22 March, commenting on the British Chancellor Gordon Brown's last budget.

Where there's a Wills, there's a…Wahey!

The Sun, 27 March, after Prince William was pictured clubbing in Bournemouth with attractive girls.

The Day Dr No said Yes

The Leader in the *Guardian*, 27 March, after Ian Paisley agreed with Gerry Adams a date for a new power-sharing agreement.

I Went to Iran and All I Got Was this Lousy Suit

The Sun, 5 April 2007, after the British naval captees were given suits by Iran on release, and playing on a traditional T-shirt slogan.

God Wants His Ball Back

The Sun, 26 April, on the death of the English football hero Alan Ball.

Harry Potty

Daily Mirror, 21 July, as millions of Harry Potter fans stormed bookshops as the final instalment of J K Rowling's series went on sale.

Not a Drop to Drink

Daily Mail, 23 July, reporting on the devastating floods that hit central England and which left thousands of homes without running water. The headline draws on Samuel Coleridge's *Rime of the Ancient Mariner*: 'Water, water, everywhere, Nor any drop to drink.'

More Bulldog Than Poodle

The Washington Post, 31 July 2007, on Gordon Brown's first official meeting with George Bush after becoming Prime Minister. Reports suggested that the two leaders shared little of the camaraderie which characterized the President's relationship with Tony Blair, as well as a distinct stiffness on the part of Mr Brown.

words in the spotlight

swive

It is never safe to say that a word has disappeared from public view. In January 2007, it was announced that in the course of preparing a scholarly edition of the writings of King Charles I, a British academic, Sarah Poynting, had made a surprising discovery. Her work on letters written in code during the King's captivity revealed a surprising item of vocabulary.

The letter in question had been written in 1648 to Jane Whorwood, the stepdaughter of one of Charles's courtiers, who was proposing to visit the King in Carisbrooke Castle where he was imprisoned. Charles wrote that the permission for the visit would be easily obtained, but that it would be more difficult to speak privately. The next sentence was written in his personal cipher, and has previously been decoded as 'Yet I imagine there is one way possible that you may get answering from me.' Dr Poynting realized that 'answering' could only be right if Charles had made three mistakes in coding the word. Working on the text (which went on to suggest a way in which Jane could be admitted secretly to his apartments), she came up with an alternative reading: 'I imagine that there is one way possible that you may get a swiving from me.'

Swive is a Germanic word which in Old English meant 'move in a course, sweep'. In the specialized sense considered here, which goes back to late Middle English, it might be described as an early 's-word'. It is a blunt term for 'have sex with', and appears in Chaucer's bawdy *Miller's Tale*: 'Thus swyued was this Carpenteris wyf'. At the end of the 17th century, in the reign of Charles II, it was used by the notorious Lord Rochester in his poem 'A Ramble in St James's Park': 'Footmen, fine fops, do here arrive, and here promiscuously they swive.'

While 'swive' was current in the 17th century, it is an unexpected word to find as used by Charles the Martyr King, a devoted husband with no reputation for the licentious lifestyle that was to characterize his son. The revelation ensured that this bit of scholarly transcription became a news story and that a once ancient word enjoyed a brief moment of unlikely notoriety.

11

Green: The New Black

Had I been editing *Time* magazine I would not have opted for the 'you' in YouTube as Person of the Year—although that was very clever. No, I'd have run an all-green *Time* cover under the headline, 'Color of the Year.' Because I think that the most important thing to happen this past year was that living and thinking 'green'—that is, mobilizing for the environmental/energy challenge we now face—hit Main Street.

Thomas Friedman in *The New York Times*, 22 December 2006.

Thomas Friedman is not alone in recognizing the exponential increase of 'green' awareness in the 21st century. From a position of vague recognition of the green movement—or alternatively a far more conscious rejection of it by those who, in Friedman's words again, considered it too 'liberal', 'tree-hugging', or 'girly-man'—we have reached in the 21st century a tipping point which is arguably more dramatic than any more transitory political happening. Living ethically in a way that serves the environment rather than exploits it is now an imperative rather than a simple personal choice. The environmental movement has been legitimized by local, national, and international government in a quite unprecedented way, and their aims are far-reaching. In the US military, for example, the

Pentagon has enlisted **Green Hawks** who are empowered with the task of improving energy efficiency in the army.

The dramatic embrace of environmental endeavour has been accompanied by an array of new words and terms. As never before, we are being encouraged to **reduce**, **reuse**, and **recycle** to avoid having to **pay as you throw**, while being careful not to be branded an **eco-smugster**. Many such new words and phrases will fail to achieve regular use, but some are likely to prove long-lived, and in fact may survive to describe the very age in which we now live.

In his 2007 Reith lectures, Jeffrey Sachs talked about the 'challenge of the **Anthropocene**' (*anthro* being Greek for 'man'). This has been proposed as a name for a new geological epoch, distinct from past periods in recognizing the 'central role' which human activity now plays in shaping both ecology and geology. The naming of an Anthropocene epoch was first proposed by Nobel Prize winner Paul Crutzen and Eugene Stoermer in 2000. They suggested that the latter 18th century should be considered the time of the onset of the Anthropocene. Professor Sachs' endorsement of the term can only increase the chances that it will be accepted, although it would appear that the exact starting date of the new epoch could remain a point of conjecture for some time to come.

While the world of politics exists on rather less than a geological timescale, nevertheless it is proving an interesting source of environmental language. The Labour Party's election manifesto of 1997 was already mentioning global warming when it proposed a target for reduced carbon dioxide (CO_2) emissions. **Carbon** soon became a shorthand for carbon dioxide, and in March 2007 the *Observer* reported that government policy now includes a bill recommending that a national **carbon budget** should be prepared. This could be used to provide strict quotas, or **carbon allowances**, for industrial greenhouse gases. In such a scheme, companies would be allowed a fixed number of **carbon credits**. Already **carbon trading** schemes are in place in some countries to allow higher polluters to obtain credits from companies that produce fewer greenhouse gases. Reductions in emissions now also have an associated **carbon value**.

Similarly, US politicians are now eager to publicize their green credentials. The *Los Angeles Times* reported in March 2007 that the Governor of California Arnold Schwarzenegger was trying to reduce his **carbon footprint** by buying trees for planting. The trees will absorb CO_2, acting as a **carbon sink**. This practice is known as **carbon offsetting**. Ironically many of these terms have been popularized by an ex-politician, former US Vice-President Al Gore. Gore's SOS (Save Our Selves) campaign to raise environmental awareness has included the 2006 documentary *An Inconvenient Truth* and the Live Earth concerts in July 2007. He has been criticized by some for his own travelling campaign's carbon footprint, although in the *Daily Telegraph* in April 2007 the environmental consultant for Live Earth confirmed that 'the concerts themselves would be **carbon neutral**'. Reflecting the new climate, the *New Oxford American Dictionary* also announced 'carbon neutral' as their word of the year for 2006.

Current terminology relating to carbon dioxide has now proliferated across all areas of society. In February 2007 the *Evening Standard* urged its readers to consider 'Twenty ways YOU can cut your carbon footprint'. Now synonymous with one's effect on the environment, a carbon footprint is a measure of the amount of CO_2 produced by an organization or individual which burns fossil fuels.

Websites provide **carbon calculators** to allow individuals to calculate their own footprint, or **carbon weight**. *The Low Carbon Diet* by Polly Ghazi and Rachel Lewis, published in May 2007, details a programme for readers to reduce their **carbon calories**.

As the debate on climate change continues to rage, **eco-doomsters** interpret every warm spell as proof of global warming. They monitor **climate canaries** closely. In 2006 the American Dialect Society referred to a climate canary as a 'species whose poor health or declining numbers hint at a larger environmental catastrophe on the horizon'. While only runners-up in the Society's word of the year poll, the canaries were at least rewarded with winning the 'most useful' category. It is predicted that climate change could cause different areas to become drier, wetter, or even colder, and in November 2002 the *New York Times* reported suggestions to call some of these stranger effects **global weirding**. Well-publicized examples of global weirding are the **drunken trees** of Alaska and Siberia. In 2006 *An Inconvenient Truth* showed images of healthy trees falling as the permafrost in which they are rooted starts to melt. According to the *Guardian* in December 2003, another environmental change is that 'each year less light reaches the surface of the Earth'. It is thought to be caused by an increase in particulates such as black carbon in the atmosphere, as a result of human activity. The report referred to this effect as **global dimming**.

Industries and companies whose practices are viewed as being environmentally unsound have now become targets for linguistic attacks from the environmental lobby. If thought responsible for placing positive 'spin' on processes that are harmful to the environment, they may well be accused of **greenwashing**. The Oxford English Corpus describes how **eco-porn** is the term of choice for 'a corporate advertisement that extols the company's environmental record even though the company is well known to carelessly exploit the environment'.

Possible solutions to the environmental issues we now face seem to grow in number on a daily basis, and as they do so a whole new crop of neologisms are emerging. For the committed environmentalist, **Freeganism** is a possible action to follow. **Freegans** (a portmanteau word formed from 'free' and 'vegan') describe themselves as avoiding 'buying anything to the greatest degree we are able'. They hope that by boycotting the economic system, they will help to support ethical considerations. If this sounds too extreme a change, then why not consider becoming a **hyper-miler**? Hyper-miling is the taking of extreme measures in order to achieve maximum fuel efficiency in a car—these measures may include driving without heating even in freezing temperatures, and avoiding the use of brakes wherever possible. Drivers of hybrid-technology vehicles are becoming increasingly enthusiastic about their low levels of fuel consumption. Some urban planners now subscribe to **green urbanism**, and try to reduce the ecological footprint of a city as it develops. They may want to consider including **biotecture** in their plans: in 2007 a team at MIT produced a house 'constructed almost entirely from living trees and plants'.

Of course, despite our best efforts to be **eco-savvy**, many fear that we may have already damaged our own planet beyond repair. As a consequence, the quest for a **Goldilocks planet** 'whose size, temperature and composition are all just right for life' (*Newsweek*, June 2002) continues. The discovery of a planet orbiting the star Gliese 581 in April 2007 has drawn a number of excited headlines, and has been described by the BBC as 'the most Earth-like planet outside our Solar System to date'. We should hope that the planet named

Gliese 581c is not **plutoed**: a verb that came into (and quickly fell out of) currency in 2006 following the demotion of the planet Pluto to what was termed a **dwarf planet** or **planemo**. If the direst climate-change predictions prove not to be **eco-scams**, we may need to visit it.

12

Bubbling Under in 2007

Each *language report* has included a collection of words which are being monitored by dictionary-makers for signs of staying power. Together they represent an eclectic mix of the serious and the trivial. The words of the moment from 2007 are no exception. Many may prove so ephemeral that they will be gone 12 months from now, while others already show signs of semi-permanence and enough persistence to warrant inclusion in the next Oxford dictionaries. Whatever their longevity, each of them contributes something to the composite linguistic snapshot of their time.

Today's preoccupations are clear. Technology (its abuses as well as its advantages), the culture of speed, new social demographics, and citizen journalism are all themes that continue strongly in this year's coinages. While last year's *mandals* are gone, in name at least, the **heely** takes over, and yesterday's *dark tourist* may be today's **poorist**. *Kangaerobics* meanwhile looks to be threatened by the latest gym craze of **chaos training**, and such terms are likely to keep on coming, for emerging more strongly this year is the desire for physical perfection. The catalyst for so much exercise- and fitness-focused vocabulary in recent years—the quest for bodily improvement—is nothing new. The striving for **size zero** and **thinspiration**, however, is looking to be a productive if undesirable source of new terms.

The following words are, to borrow a term from the music charts, 'bubbling under' the surface of mainstream English. Usage will, as ever, be their final arbiter.

Beckham rule: a concession made to each football team in America's major league soccer game: they may take on one player whose salary is excluded from salary cap rules which limit teams to an overall salary of around £1m per year. The rule came into effect when David Beckham was signed up by the Los Angeles Galaxy team in a move reported to earn him over $250 million over five years.

bipodding: listening to a music player with someone else. The term comes from the idea of two ('bi-') people using an iPod.

blokarting: the new sport of 'land yachting', which involves steering a go-cart which has a sail attached and is thus wind-powered. Originating in New Zealand, it is the latest in a line of fusion sports which also includes **octopushing**: underwater hockey in which two teams compete to push a 'squid' (the puck) across the bottom of a pool with a short stick.

burkini: a swimming costume that conforms to Islamic standards of modest dress for women, consisting of trousers and a long-sleeved tunic with a hijab style of headscarf.

chaos training™: the latest in new exercise routines to pack out New York's gyms. The training, which its creators claim is loosely based on chaos theory, is based on the idea of randomly varying exercise routines so that the body's muscles never know what to expect. The training might include the 'inchworm walk' or the 'body drag' (in which the exerciser shuffles along the floor on their stomach pushing a heavy ball).

eckham rule **bipodding** blokarting **clickprint** digilanti er

clickprint: an individual's pattern of online usage—in other words their online 'footprint'. It follows the earlier **clickstream**, which is the virtual path taken by Web surfers.

CRAGGER: a member of a carbon rationing action group, whose aim is to reduce substantially the amount of harmful CO_2 they and others release into the atmosphere.

crowdsourcing: a version of outsourcing in business, involving the use of large groups of amateurs outside an organization to test a product or to perform other work, usually for a fraction of the usual cost.

digilanti: volunteers who try to keep the Internet free from spam and scams. The term is a blend of 'digital' and 'vigilante'.

empty-chairing: the practice, used by TV and radio presenters, of drawing attention to the fact that a politician has refused to appear for an interview. Sometimes the camera shows the physical evidence of an empty chair, while the term also denotes the repetition by presenters that a minister was asked to comment but declined. The British Defence Secretary Des Browne was the target of empty-chairing when he failed to comment on the selling of their stories by soldiers who had been held captive in Iran.

flipping: buying a highly desirable fashion item and reselling it quickly on the auction site eBay for a big profit.

ghostriding the whip: dancing on the bonnet of one's car with the stereo cranked up to maximum volume and with the car set to 'drive'. This is the latest craze in the established black cultural

hairing ghostriding the whip Beckham rule bipodding bl

phenomenon on the West Coast of America known as **hyphy** (short for 'hyperactive'): a style of dance and music associated with hip-hop culture. A **whip**, in hip-hop slang, is a car. The idea was given a big push when the rapper E-40 made a track called *Tell Me When To Go* which includes the lyrics:

> Ghost-ride the whip
> …Put your stunna shades on
> Now… Gas, brake, dip, dip
> Shake them dreads
> Let me see you show your grill.

E-40, Warner Bros label, 2006.

gingerism: prejudice against red-heads. The word came to the fore in Britain in the summer of 2007 after a red-haired family claimed to have been driven from their home as a result of harassment. Prince Harry was also said to have suffered verbal teasing in the army because of his hair-colour, allegedly earning him the nickname 'Ginger Bullet Magnet'.

go-bag: a bag containing clothes and other essential items should a person need to evacuate their home quickly in the event of an emergency such as a terrorist attack or flood.

hauterfly: a fashion guru who is very much part of the industry's social scene. The term is a blend of 'haute couture' and 'butterfly' or 'gadfly'.

> Snooping Around Hauterflies' Homes! Fashion voyeurs rejoice! *Elle Décor's* September Glamour issue takes a beyond-the-front-row look at the homes of some of the industry's best-known bold-faced names.

Fashionweekdaily.com, July 2005.

phy hauterfly gingerism go-bag item girl meh meshing

heely: a branded training shoe with one or more wheels fixed in the heel part of the shoe so that the wearer can move more quickly. Various wheel configurations are available, each allowing different stunts. **Heeling** is considered to be a form of skating and is banned in the US by some shopping malls and schools. The craze swept through the UK in 2007—the home video site YouTube has plenty of footage of expert **heelying**.

item girl: an established colloquial term in India for a woman ('item boys' are less common) who sings an 'item song' or 'item number': an upbeat dance or song that is interpolated in a Bollywood film but which has no connection with the plot.

meh: the new verbal 'shrug', the latest equivalent to 'whatever', and meaning boring, rubbish, or simply not worth the effort. It is widely used in blogs, chatrooms, and messageboards, as a pithy indication of nonchalance.

> No one is quite sure where it comes from. Graeme Diamond, principal editor of the new word group at the Oxford English Dictionary, says it's not yet suitable for the OED, but he does have a "meh" file, and the first recorded print usage occurred in the Edmonton Sun newspaper in Canada in 2003: "Ryan Opray got voted off *Survivor*. Meh."
>
> *The Guardian*, March 2007.

meshing: a trend among American newlyweds of blending their surnames to avoid the perceived sexism of the wife taking her husband's name. (See 'Language on the Horizon' for how celebrities are doing it, pp 74–5.)

item girl hauterfly gingerism go-bag meh meshing ite

mesicopter: a helicopter which measures approximately 1 cm wide and which is being developed for NASA as a means of monitoring weather. Other NASA ideas and projects to aid human exploration include an **entomopter**—a robot which can fly or crawl to investigate new terrain—and a **starshade** which blocks out light from the stars to enable better imaging of other planets.

mis mem: a 'misery memoir', often the story of a celebrity's difficult life before they achieved fame. In 2007 *Publishers Weekly* reported that the publishers Hodder Headline had introduced a new sub-genre: 'sports misery', featuring the hard-luck stories of faded footballers.

mobile clubbing: a concept in clubbing which has attracted a cult following, whereby a mobile 'club' is organized via the Internet and clubbers gather together in a public place such as a railway station and dance wildly to their own MP3 players.

mojo: an amateur journalist who uses their mobile phone to gather and disseminate news from within a community or from a live event.

mumblecore: a genre of US indie films which are strongly naturalistic, usually low-budget, and which document the lives and loves of young twenty-somethings. A tongue-in-cheek term, it alludes to the 'mumbling' of the characters in such films as they act out their often mundane lives.

nurikabe: a Japanese logic puzzle which is the latest to make its way into British newspapers in the wake of the highly successful *sudoku* puzzles and the more recent *futoshikis* and *kakuros*. The name in Japanese folklore refers to an invisible wall which blocks paths and roads and upon which delays in travel are blamed.

OCPO (an acronym for Organized Crime Prevention Order): a kind of super-ASBO which targets people in organized crime, especially those who perpetrate drug or people trafficking and money-laundering. Because of the difficulty in proving such activity, OCPO civil orders require a lower level of proof than the 'beyond reasonable doubt' of criminal law.

olderpreneur: a person who starts up their own business in their late 40s or 50s. It follows on from various new groups identified and labelled in the 2000s, including **alterpreneurs** and **soul proprietors**, both of whom pursue an alternative, less work-driven lifestyle, and their opposite, **upshifters**, who return to high-living having experimented with **downshifting**.

peerents: parents who behave like their children's peers (or who treat their kids like their own peers) in a form of collaborative parenting. The term may well be one which, for all its coverage, never quite takes off.

ping: a US term for a microwave meal, part of **ping cuisine**.

poorism: travel that includes tours of slums or dangerous urban neighbourhoods. The term has a derogatory edge: such visits are seen by some as unethical and voyeuristic.

> Is poverty tourism—"poorism" they call it—exploration or exploitation?

> From an article in the *Smithsonian* magazine titled 'Next Stop, Squalor', March 2007.

prevenge: the act of getting one's retaliation in first. The word has been around since the late 1990s but is coming into wider use now, particularly in blogs and message-boards. A similar recent coinage is **precrimination**: a recrimination made in advance of an anticipated event or outcome—in effect, a **pre-mortem**.

punch one's ticket (US)**:** to do or achieve something that guarantees a next step in progression.

read-dating: the new version of speed-dating, but instead of personal details the attendees at read-dating parties discuss books with a prospective date for three minutes before moving on to the next person.

> In quick succession I meet Richard, who has picked Hyperion…; Adam, who's never been read-dating before and thought this would be easier than going to a pub; and John, a slick and slightly smug barrister, who cheerfully admits he is looking for 'a shag'.
>
> Sarah Hughes in 'Yes, you can judge a bloke by his cover' in the *Observer*, March 2006.

shop-dropping: a tactic used by artists and activists to covertly place objects in retail stores. Dropped objects are usually versions of consumer products which have been altered or recreated as a critical gesture against the normal retail experience.

snap dance: a slow dance to hip hop music with lots of finger-snapping. It has been popularized by artists and groups such as Dem Franchize Boyz and D4L, and has its roots in the 70s Californian dance style, **poplocking**, in which dancers contract and relax

their muscles in quick succession in order to cause a jerk in their body, referred to as a 'pop' or a 'hit'.

spanador: a cross between a spaniel and a Labrador and the latest in a long line of dog name 'blends', including labradoodles, cockapoos, and schnoodles (poodles and schnauzers).

tombstoning: an extreme sport which involves jumping off a high point such as a sea cliff or bridge into water. In 2007 a number of deaths and injuries from tombstoning brought the term into unwelcome relief.

tweet: a short posting or message sent by **Twitter**, a new commu-nications gateway, to a mobile phone or website. It is known as a form of **microblogging**, a mini-blog about what the sender is doing right at that moment, that can be posted to a mobile phone as well as online.

urbeach: an urban beach, and a trend that began with the Paris Plage, a section of land by the Seine which the authorities cover with sand and furnish with deckchairs every summer. New urbeaches are planned for Bristol and Birmingham (rumoured to be called Plage Brum), among other cities.

vishing: This new breed of Internet fraud is a blend of VOIP (Voice Over Internet Protocol, denoting Internet telephony) and 'phishing', the obtaining of passwords and other personal informa-tion illicitly. **Vishers** target individuals by telephoning them via a recorded message which asks the victim to ring their credit-card provider to verify account information. When they ring the number to authenticate, the visher captures the number and uses it to make fraudulent purchases. **Smishing**, meanwhile, is another new offshoot, and involves 'phishing' via mobile phone text (SMS) message.

Wiimote: a motion-sensitive remote control used with the cult Nintendo Wii video game. The Wii games themselves have been wildly successful, distinguished from others by their motion-sensitive technology that requires players to act out the movements of the character they are role-playing. The resulting physical work-out, much applauded by health-watchers, has also given rise to the terms **wiiflexes**, and **Wii elbow**: arm pain caused by excessive use. Further 'Wii-' compounds are only to be expected.

wilfing: aimless Internet surfing. The term is said to originate in an acronym formed from the phrase 'What Was I Looking For?'

Wyatting: putting a very obscure track on an Internet jukebox to deliberately disconcert other more mainstream pub-goers. The term comes from the name of Robert Wyatt, whose LP *Dondestan* is often used for this purpose. The term, coined by an English teacher, appeared in some blogs and music magazines in 2007. However short-lived, it is a good example of the power of the blog in spreading neologisms.

800lb gorilla: a powerful or influential factor in something. The term is also used as the latest equivalent of the **elephant in the room** or the **moose on the table**, both of which mean the same: something which it is impossible to overlook but which no one wants to talk about. The idea of the gorilla may derive from the joke 'Where does an 800lb gorilla sit? Wherever he likes!'.

13

The Words of the Years

The words which enter the *Oxford English Dictionary* every year can be as telling as the history books about the time which produced them. Each *language report* has selected a single word from each of the last hundred years which captures some of the spirit of that time—so, for example *tailspin* from 1917, *beatnik* from 1958, or *flower children* from 1967—all chime with the feel of their respective era.

Many of those words are still in use, having never changed their meaning. They surprise us in their earliness—*celeb* (1913), *spliff* (1936), *fast food* (1951), and *gangland* (1912) are still very much in currency. Some may have faded from view for a time, but have been resurrected to fit the new realities we live in: a Tolkienesque *hobbit* became in 2005 the name for an apparently new species of human discovered on a remote Indonesian island, while *Big Brother*, coined by Orwell in 1949, has taken on a new life thanks to TV voyeurism. Others still may survive as linguistic time capsules, resonating with the feel of their age—few of us can fail to conjure up a particular era in our minds at the mention of *demob*, *bebop*, *hula hoop*, *alcopop*, *ladette*, and *glasnost*.

There are different categories at work too. *Chav*, a century-old word, returned with such a force that compounds and derivatives—

chavtastic, *chavsters*, and *chavettes*, for example—emerged at lightning speed. *Sudoku*, on the other hand, stands by itself: it is the name, taken wholesale from another language without any adjustment or development, of something that didn't exist before, but which in due course will be as familiar as *crossword* is now. *Surge* is different again: it is a standard term born in the 16th century. In the 21st century, however, it has acquired a new and very particular military meaning.

The following collections of words by decade represent the choices of the various *language reports*. Together they form an illuminating mosaic of a hundred years of neologisms, and of the society which created them.

1900–09

- cornflake
- jazz
- muckraking
- plane
- speed limit
- suffragette
- teddy bear
- telephone box
- whizzo
- egghead
- Realpolitik

tnik gangland alcopop Sudoku surge tailspin beatnik ga

1910–19

ace [pilot]

blues

civvy street

crossword

phone number

shell shock

tailspin

talkies

trench fever

U-boat

celeb

gene

ceasefire

1920–29

boogie-woogie

bright young thing

Charleston

demob

fridge

gangland

hem-line

nail varnish

perm

Wall Street Crash

pop

avant-garde

Big Apple

1930–39

apparatchik

evacuee

facelift

Gestapo

hobbit

Mickey Mouse

pizza

private eye

It-girl

dumb down

spliff

cheeseburger

Blitzkrieg

1940–49

antibiotic

apartheid

atom bomb

bebop

bikini

blitz

cappuccino

cold war

garden gnome

Gulag

Molotov cocktail

New Look

nylons

TV

mobile phone

DNA

Wonderbra

Big Brother

brainwashing

1950–59

beatnik

cruise missile

double helix

hula hoop

McCarthyism

nuclear disarmament

rock and roll

seatbelt [in cars]

UFO
fast food
Generation X
hippy
non-U
boogie
sexy
psychedelic

1960–69

bossa nova
Dalek
flower children
game show
garden centre
generation gap
microchip
miniskirt
peacenik
reggae
skyjack
spacewalk
acid
love-in

1970–79

Big Mac

breakfast television

Watergate (and with it all things '–gate')

green

hot pants

microwave

Page Three girl

palimony

Trekkie

F-word

punk

detox

karaoke

1980–89

email

glasnost

latte

lovely jubbly

Prozac

road rage

spin doctor

velvet revolution

power-dressing

toyboy

hip-hop

beatbox

OK yah

double-click

virtual reality

gangsta

1990–99

alcopop

blog

Botox

dotcom

ethnic cleansing

Google

home page

ladette

text message

hotdesking

having it large

glasnost road rage **spin doctor** OK yah **dotcom** hotdeski

The Word of the 21st Century

In the closing years of the 2000s, the challenge is to find the word
which offers us some kind of shorthand for the first decade of
the new century. Any single item chosen will of course be one-
dimensional: the last eight years have seen major conflict in the
Middle East, worldwide terrorist attacks including those of
September 11, 2001, the effects of a catastrophic tsunami in South
East Asia, the battering of New Orleans by Hurricane Katrina, the
signature of a historic power-sharing agreement in Northern
Ireland, and the ending of political terms of office in major Western
powers including Britain, the US, and France. Socially, the 2000s
have been marked by debates on healthcare, gay marriage, obesity,
terrorism, fundamentalism, and human rights, while technological
progress has been led by the advent of broadband capability and
mobile phone communication. The new words coined amidst these
happenings together create an accurate picture of a point in time:
to choose one is necessarily subjective. The process of deliberating,
however, can be instructive.

For this fifth *language report*, Oxford University Press is inviting
readers to select the word which represents for them the events or
moods of the century so far.

The following words, which include the choice for the year 2007,
footprint, offer a partial snapshot of the decade so far. Not all
are brand new. Some are older words which have found a new
and high-profile context. There are many more possibilities.
Readers can go to *www.askoxford.com* to nominate one of these,
or their own.

rint **bling** chav **axis of evil** tsunami **Hurricane Katrina** fo

2000–2007

axis of evil

This term, first used by George W. Bush in his State of the Union address in January 2002, came to be shorthand in his administration's rhetoric about the threat of terrorism and weapons of mass destruction from an 'axis' or group of countries which included Iraq, Iran, and North Korea. Coined by Bush's speechwriter David Frum, who took as his inspiration a speech by Franklin D. Roosevelt some sixty years earlier, it was a phrase which became synonymous with the US's articulation of the need for dislodging Saddam Hussein.

bling

Although coined in the late nineties by the US rapper B.G. (Baby Gangsta), 'bling' is for many the word of the early noughties, denoting a celebrity-obsessed culture intent on being as flashy as those whom it idolized. Said to be the representation of light reflecting off diamonds, the term moved from hip-hop into mass culture with dramatic speed. 'Bling' has today lost some of its popularity—in 2005 MTV showed a satirical cartoon which charted the demise of the word, from its hip beginnings to its use by those who were decidedly not street-wise. It ended with the caption 'RIP bling, 1997–2004'.

chav

The word 'chav' offered in 2004–5 a near-perfect example of the speed at which today's new words can spread. In this case the word was a revival of a much older term—one which began in Romany use in the middle of the 19th century. Very few of us will have heard

int **bling** chav **axis of evil** tsunami **Hurricane Katrina** fo of it until the website *chavscum.com* brought it back into parlance and began an upsurge of distaste at a 'burgeoning peasant under-class'. Within weeks the word was being noted with alarm in liberal circles, and used to varying degrees of humour and distaste by the public at large.

If today the term is losing some of its pejorative edge, it is nonethe-less still very much at the vanguard of a resurgence of an 'us and them' mentality which has characterized the opening decade of the century (see 'Us and Them', pp 47–54).

bovvered

When Tony Blair appeared in a Comic Relief comedy sketch with the character of Lauren from *The Catherine Tate Show*, the catch-phrase 'Am I bovvered?' turned official. Days later it was repeated with hilarity in Prime Minister's Question Time in the House of Commons, with David Cameron expressing mock incredulity that the Chancellor and would-be next PM Gordon Brown 'bothered talking to the Prime Minister; he is not bovvered any more'.

'Bovvered' has been repeated by the media as a neat shorthand for Britain's ASBO-deserving couldn't-care-less adolescents. It took over from Vicky Pollard's (from the comedy *Little Britain*) catchphrase 'wha'ev-ah', seen as the ultimate teenage opt-out from communi-cating (and from proper English).

It may well prove that Tony Blair's embracing of the term will render it so uncool as to make it henceforth unappealing to those who have been using it with relish.

9/11

The language used to express or designate certain events can be as powerful a distillation of history as photographs or film. The spontaneous choice of the date 9/11 as the immediate reference point for the terrorist attacks against America in 2001 is likely to retain these associations forever. Even in the UK, 9/11—which has supplanted the early British equivalent September 11th—is the shorthand of choice for the events of that single day. The repercussions of the attacks have resonated throughout the years since, and many might consider them to be the catalyst for a chain of political and social events which have dominated the decade.

SARS and bird flu

In spite of the cold unmemorability of the acronym, SARS (severe acute respiratory syndrome) gripped the public imagination in 2004 as the latest threat to public health. So readily was it adopted in Britain that the tabloid newspapers felt confident enough to use it in punning headlines such as 'SARS WARS'. The language of disease has long been affected by anxiety and superstition— perhaps by bowing to the language of science we reassure ourselves that we know what is at work so that we can increase our **biosecurity** (another contender). In our minds, however, it is 'bird flu' that is ringing the alarm bells.

sex up

Contesting for the phrases of 2003 were **dodgy dossier**, **weapons of mass destruction**, and **sexing up**. Unusually, they all came from a single context, notably a briefing document prepared for Tony Blair's government on Iraq's 'Infrastructure of Concealment,

Deception, and Intimidation'. The dossier was the basis for the government's rationale for the subsequent invasion of Iraq.

It was Channel 4 News which coined the phrase 'dodgy dossier' after it revealed that much of the document had taken arguments from various unattributed sources. It was a phrase much repeated when the weapons of mass destruction (**WMDs**) proved elusive.

Sex up, meaning to make more appetizing, dramatic, or indeed sexy, came into greater currency thanks to a BBC report by the journalist Andrew Gilligan that British intelligence reports on Iraq had been 'sexed up' in order to justify war. The truth or otherwise of this was a major talking point in the Hutton Inquiry which was set up to investigate the death of David Kelly, an employee of the Ministry of Defence who was named as the source for a number of Andrew Gilligan's statements.

The phrase 'sexing up' was soon applied to any number of contexts, from one's body or bedroom to further political documents where spin was suspected.

footprint

The 21st century has seen the prolific 'greening' of our language as well as our culture (see pp 126–132). Today, phrases such as 'reduce your footprint' require no glossing—the new imperative (one which for many scientists has been expressed far too late) is to minimize our impact on our planet. 'Footprints' come in many forms: they may be carbon, green, or ecological (eco-), while we may use a **footprint calculator** to measure our impact on our natural resources. Ecological **footprint analysis** attempts to measure the human demand upon nature.

The frequency with which 'footprint' now evokes an environmental context can be measured by the Oxford English Corpus. At the beginning of the 2000s, 'carbon' and 'ecological' scarcely featured on the linguistic map for 'footprint': today they are among its most frequent companions, along with the verb 'reduce'.

bowser

The floods which hit northern and southern Britain in the summer of 2007 brought the hitherto rather specialized word 'bowser' into common parlance. The term was named after the American inventor of the storage petrol pump, Sylvanus Bowser, whose portable machines became indispensable for refuelling airplanes during the Second World War. Over time, the term 'bowser' became extended to include machines which supply water on construction sites or in the military. Few could have predicted their value in 2007 when they brought uncontaminated water to thousands of flood-affected Britons.

And a few more contenders...

size zero (see p 82)

podcasting (see p 104)

surge (see pp 67–9)

truthiness (see pp 83–4)

Ground Zero (see p 12)

er truthiness footprint analysis surge bowser footprint c

Index